A Way in the Wilderness

A Way in the Wilderness

A Commentary on the Rule of Benedict for the Physically and Spiritually Imprisoned

James Bishop

continuum

Published by the Continuum International Publishing Group

The Tower Building
11 York Road
London
SE1 7NX

80 Maiden Lane
Suite 704
New York
NY 10038

www.continuumbooks.com

First published 2012

British Library Cataloguing-in-Publication Data
A catalogue record for this book is available from the British Library.

ISBN: PB: 978-1-4411-5115-5

Typeset by Fakenham Prepress Solutions, Fakenham, Norfolk NR21 8NN
Printed and bound in India

Dedication

This commentary is dedicated to the following:

Fr. John Main, OSB, founder of the World Community for Christian Meditation: for reigniting the tradition that has brought me peace and tranquility.

Fr. Laurence Freeman, OSB, Director of the World Community for Christian Meditation: for seemingly endless guidance on the path of peace.

Sister Benita Lankford: for braving the razor wire and steel to come to a prison and teach us hardened criminals how to meditate.

Sisters Christine, Caroline, and Diana, the chaplains at the prison: for bringing Sr. Benita to us.

Jennifer Greenleaves: who proofread the manuscript, tirelessly hunting typographical and grammatical errors to the death.

Victims of crime all over the world: for my prayer that the love of God will heal them of their physical and mental scars.

The prisoners of the world: for my prayer that God may lead you along the path of healing and reconciliation.

Contents

CONTENTS

Foreword

The first time I went to visit a prison I had an uncanny feeling of familiarity. Eventually it dawned on me that it was because it seemed like a monastery. It was enclosed, institutional, highly structured. You were either a visitor or an inmate and of course these two ways of being inside gave very different perspectives. The deeper similarity is that these unnatural or at least unconventional conditions – different in that one is freely chosen and the other not – both hold great potential. Like any situation we find ourselves in, its meaning depends on what we make of it. Deprivation, exclusion, solitude can be destructive and make us desperate. Or they can be redemptive, purifying and form an opportunity for spiritual flourishing – an ascesis such as the early Christian monks, the fathers of the desert, some of whom were themselves former criminals, would have embraced willingly.

Dostoevsky said that the test of a civilization is found in the nature of the prisons it runs. Some are so inhumane as to be in themselves a crime against humanity. Others sin against the people they are incarcerating merely by their degree of impersonality and callousness or for failing in giving effective protection against the violent and abusive inmates. Some perhaps do take their role as centres of rehabilitation seriously. I have not visited a prison anywhere that seemed to me to do this properly although I have met many remarkable people working in the prison system who do work to help the inmates change for the better and who radiate a deeply loving and wise humane spirit. I think of the sister who was chaplain in James Bishop's prison, a handicapped older woman who had an impossible job responsible for thousands of inmates. Yet like David against the system, she fought hard for those she was able to help. She worked to establish lines of spiritual support that helped at least a few to rise above their ordeal and find God as few people, unable to handle the gift of freedom, manage to do on the outside.

On the day I visited the prison to see the regular meditation group and receive James' final oblation, she greeted us with the announcement that the whole prison had been shut down. This was an absolute sanction that even the most authoritarian monastery never imposes, forcing each inmate to remain quiet in his cell. The reasons for this might be a riot, a breach of the rules or just a shortage of guards on that shift. We felt disappointed and frustrated as we had driven more than a hundred miles on a very hot day. Then she told us she was working on the officer in charge and that he had given an exceptional permission for the meditation group to meet and the oblation to take place. We went to thank the officer who greeted us like a walking armoury but was a man of unexpected sensitivity. I thanked him and said how moved I was to meditate with the prisoners and how receptive they were and how research has shown that meditation in prison helps not only the prisoners but the whole ethos of the institution. He agreed but added as a caution, as we left, to remember that I would be likely to see the best of the inmates and, of them, their best part.

Maybe this was true of James Bishop but I was impressed by his friendships with the others, his lack of complaining and his faith. In my conversations in prison with James I was always struck by his humour and lack of self-pity. He took his Benedictine oblate novitiate very seriously and his final oblation on that auspicious day, celebrated with about fifty of his fellow inmates, was a truly sacred event. I am always struck by this sacred act of self-giving (oblation means 'offering') at final oblations within our monastery without walls, The World Community for Christian Meditation. But there, inside those unforgiving and impenetrable walls, it was particularly spiritual.

FOREWORD

An oblate promises to live by the spirit of the Rule of St Benedict and its precepts of stability, conversion and obedience in accordance with the conditions of their life and vocation. In our wall-less global monastery a twice-daily meditation practice is the essential bond of unity and the underlying discipline supported by the divine office (regular readings of scripture during the day) and sharing in the life and work of the community.

Because St Benedict's 'Rule' is so sensitive to exceptions it might be said that it is the exceptions to the Rule that prove its value. James had more than enough structure and regulation in prison. What he needed and found in the community and the Rule (the Rule cannot make much sense outside of a particular community and its own interpretation of it) was what is essential to it – moderation, gentleness, honesty, regular prayer, unceasing mindfulness of God's presence and our vocation to holiness. The one thing that the Rule does not make an exception to is the call to be God-centred.

They say some of the best commentaries on the Rule have been written in hotel rooms. Here is one that was written in a room while on parole. When I first read it I did not expect to find the tone of clarity, compassion and intelligence which makes it, for me, one of the best commentaries I have read. I recommend it to our meditating oblates but also to anyone who seeks God – as St Benedict says the true monk does as the first priority – and who has found in Benedict's wise and compassionate spirit a way to be free, to be fully human.

Laurence Freeman OSB

Introduction

St. Benedict was born in approximately 480 AD. The world was quite a different place at that time. The Roman Empire had just fallen, and the world was beginning to plunge into what would be called "The Dark Ages." It was a time of intellectual as well as spiritual darkness. Our time, too, could easily be called "The Dark Ages." We are now living in a time of great darkness in our faith and morals. Now more than ever, we need guidance in our lives.

For many centuries, the monks living in monasteries throughout the world have lived by the Rule of Benedict. Benedict wrote the Rule as the leader of a community of monks. He later became known as the Great Patriarch, or father, of the Western Monks.

You may be asking, "How could this Rule apply to me? I don't live in a monastery, and I'm not sure I would want to." My response is two-fold:

1. If you are physically incarcerated, living in a prison somewhere, then you live in a community in close proximity with others. This is very much like a monastery.

2. The Rule of St. Benedict can help guide us in many ways that are not immediately discernible from a cursory glance at the text. A deeper inspection of the meaning of the text can be applied to our daily lives, whether we are in a prison community, a monastery, or simply trying to live our lives in the "real world."

This book is intended for two kinds of people: those who are incarcerated in a prison, and those who are not. For the former, you will find many interesting parallels to prison life in the Rule of St. Benedict. For the latter, you will also find many interesting parallels with your daily life and struggles, and you will discover a little about prison life as well. You may discover that, in fact, you have been living in a kind of prison.

I am a Benedictine Oblate, meaning that I have taken some of the vows of a monk, but I do not live in a monastery. I took my vows of oblation while I was incarcerated. I spent ten years in a prison, and discovered the Rule of St. Benedict there. I tried to live the Rule in prison. Now that I am out of prison, I still try to live the Rule. Through the Rule and through meditation, I have come to know that I was in a self-made prison for many years, and when I was finally sent to a physical prison, I became freer than I had ever been before in my life.

A note to those who are not physically incarcerated: It has been said that, in some way, everyone is in prison. Some are physically there. Others are there in a spiritual sense. We may feel our pleas for spiritual freedom are not being heard, or we may feel that we are limited by our lack of faith. These are simply other forms of incarceration. I will try to address these as much as possible.

The time we spend in our prisons is intended to help us heal from the troubles that may have caused us to hurt others or ourselves. Living the Rule provides some catharsis in that respect, and I hope this commentary will help provide some insight into the subtler meanings of the Rule and how it can help you. Please note that I am not a spiritual master or a guru. Rather, I am a fellow traveler. You are free to join me on this journey, and hopefully we can learn from each other.

James

Use of *The Rule of St. Benedict*

There are several translations of the Rule of St. Benedict available. Some may appeal to you more than others. I know that in prison, it can be difficult to obtain even one copy of a text like this, and I am sure getting several different translations to compare is extremely difficult. I personally have used several different translations and find them each useful, so I think any translation you can get will be fine.

The version I now use is split into different "readings" each day, for an entire year. If you can obtain a copy of the Rule, I would recommend a copy like this, so that you can make a habit of reading part of it each day.

I have made an effort to discuss the shorter chapters in one piece. However, some of the chapters are quite lengthy (such as the Prologue), so I will break them down into smaller pieces.

Please note that this is not an exhaustive commentary. I have not intended to discuss special aspects of translation, original languages, or the source texts themselves. I intend this commentary to cover deeper aspects, especially as they relate to the incarcerated. There are certainly other aspects that can be gleaned from the Rule, and I do not intend to cover all of them here.

Further, the community to which I belong is centered on Christian meditation. For that reason, much of the commentary will be likewise.

All quotes from the Bible are from the Douay-Rheims version unless otherwise stated. The masculine pronoun is often used, as in the original text of the Rule of St. Benedict. However, the worldwide community of those who have chosen to live by the Rule includes persons of all genders. No disrespect is intended.

USE OF THE RULE OF ST. BENEDICT

The text quoted from the Rule is a modernized translation from "The Holy Rule of Saint Benedict" translated from the Latin by Rev. Boniface Verheyen, OSB of St. Benedict's Abbey, Atchison, Kansas, and is in the public domain (Library of Congress call number BX3004.A2). The source text was modernized to make the reading easier (i.e. words such as "thee" and "thou" were replaced, and some more archaic and difficult language was replaced with a modern equivalent).

Prologue

Listen...

It is said that the great Church patriarch Origen had decided to write a commentary on the Bible, and he started with the Gospel of St. John. Upon beginning, he realized that he could write an entire volume on just the first verse!

Though not the infallible Word of God, the beginning of the Prologue in the Rule says quite a lot as well. The first word is "listen." Listening is one of the most difficult things we ever do. I don't necessarily mean listening to someone else when they're talking to you, but rather listening to ourselves. First, it requires that we are quiet, and remaining quiet can be quite a challenge. Try it sometime for at least a few minutes. Not just being quiet with the spoken word, but quiet in our thoughts as well.

When I started meditating in prison, I soon realized that the instruction, the "how-to" was fairly simple. Doing it, however, was quite difficult. In essence, the beginning of meditation can be put simply, if a little crudely: sit down and shut up. Sitting down stills the body. Don't move around and wriggle. Just sit quietly and calmly. Shutting up means more than not speaking; it means quieting the mind. My mind races all the time. I can't seem to keep it quiet. That's OK! Your mind will do the same thing, as will everyone's. Your mind will keep trying to be active, and thoughts will come to you when you are trying to relax. This is not a failure, but an opportunity to learn to quiet them. And it takes a LOT of practice. I have been meditating for almost ten years now, and my mind still wanders every time. It is through practice that we grow. This is discipline.

Our lives can be hectic sometimes. I remember talking to my family when I was in prison, and I would try to explain how busy I was in prison. They found it quite hard to believe that someone could be busy in prison. They didn't know! There are lots of things to do, especially if we are working on making ourselves better people. With all of that hectic activity going on, we need to take some time out of each day to "listen," as the Rule says. Be quiet, be still, and listen.

In practice, I found the best times for meditation in prison were at "count" time and before morning chow (breakfast). In the institution where I spent ten years, we had a "count" at 5:00 PM, just before dinner. We all had to be quiet and stay in our cells or on our bunks while we were counted, to make sure no one had escaped. Little did they know, as I was meditating, I was escaping in my mind! I also used to wake up in the morning a few hours before everyone else, and used the quiet, alone time to meditate.

Another problem in the prison setting is that people are constantly coming by to ask you questions or talk to you. I found that if I lay down with my eyes closed and my headphones on, they would come back later. Sometimes, I wasn't even playing music in the headphones! The headphones were just to let them know that I was not to be disturbed at that time. And they worked very well.

In the prison, I was housed for a while in what was called "Administrative Segregation." We called it "the hole," and it was where they sent us when we had gotten into trouble. Maybe a fight, or one of the officers found something in your cell that you're not supposed to have. Anyway, I was in there for seven months, no time outside, no TV or radio. Nothing! The only advantage of being there was that I could meditate very well! Take some time to incorporate "listening" in your program. You'll be glad you did.

So far, we've only covered the first word of the Prologue! Let's look at the whole first paragraph.

> *Listen, my son, to the precepts of your master, and incline the ear of your heart, and cheerfully receive and faithfully execute the admonitions of your loving Father, that by the work of obedience you may return to Him from whom by the sloth of disobedience you have gone away.*

In the first paragraph, Benedict is telling us to listen to the Master's precepts. But he asks us to use the ear of our hearts. The Master's precepts are the teachings of someone who we are following. We are probably following God (or at least trying to), maybe a supervisor, and maybe in this case, Benedict as well. He is saying, "Don't just listen to what I have to say, but listen with your heart. Understand the meaning behind what I'm telling you, and the reasons why. Take it a little deeper. Read *between the lines.*"

Note also that he refers to "your loving Father." He makes a point to show that he is loving, even though the Rule may seem harsh at times. It is a "labor of obedience." It is for your own good, and a loving father would want that for you.

Some of us have had fathers who were not the greatest role models. They may be fathers in the biological sense because they were involved in our birth process, but maybe they did not raise us as good fathers would. That is not the kind of father Benedict is speaking of here. He is speaking of someone who genuinely cares for your well-being, just as a good father should.

A little should be said here about rules. We are looking at the Rule of St. Benedict, and the very concept of rules may be something you're not ready to deal with. We have had rules to follow all our lives, and admittedly we were probably never very good at following them. After all, who wants to be a follower? It may seem that some rules were made just so someone could try to have power over us. That is not the intention of the Rule of St. Benedict. If you miss a rule, or break it in some way, no one is going to be here to scold you. When it comes to changing your life, it is something you have to want to do, and you are going to be the only one to know whether you are following what the Rule tells you in any given situation. This is not an attempt to control you or make you into someone you're not. Rather, it is an attempt to help you discover who you really are.

We have all been disobedient at times. Admitting our faults and coming to terms with them is the way to heal, and grow. Let's look at another paragraph.

> *To you, therefore, my speech is now directed, who, giving up your own will, are taking up the strong and most excellent arms of obedience, to do battle for Christ the Lord, the true King.*

Here, we are preparing for a battle within, but in order to fight effectively against our own demons we must renounce our own wills, because they are links to our faults and shortcomings. At some point in our lives, especially when we are sitting in a prison cell, we have to admit that our way of doing things hasn't worked out very well. Look where it got us! If things are going to get better, if our lives are going to change for the good, then we need to change the way we do some things. We may want to do things a certain way, but that might be the wrong way. What we want is typically called our "will." We are going to have to renounce our will, just like soldiers give up their wills to the one in charge, the "shot-caller." Let's move on to the next paragraph.

> *In the first place, beg of Him by most earnest prayer, that He make perfect whatever good you do, in order that He who has been pleased to count us as His children, need never be grieved at our evil deeds. For we ought at all times to serve Him with*

> *the good things which* He *has given us, that* He *may not, like an angry father, disinherit his children, nor, like a dread lord, enraged at our evil deeds, hand us over to everlasting punishment as most wicked servants, who would not follow* H*im to glory.*

In this paragraph, we see that our actions become perfected only through God. I am reminded of the story of a Rabbi who was saying his Passover prayers. After saying the prayers, he asked God who in the village had said the Passover prayers the best. God answered that there was a peasant who lived just down the road from the synagogue who had said the Passover prayers most perfectly. The Rabbi was shocked, thinking that he himself should have said them better than anyone else in the village. After all, he was the Rabbi! He went to see the peasant, and after being invited in, he asked the peasant man how he made his Passover prayers. The peasant replied, "Forgive me, Rabbi, for I do not know how to say them properly." The Rabbi asked again, "How did you say them?" The peasant looked to the ground and replied, "I just said the Hebrew alphabet, and I asked God to rearrange the letters into the perfect prayer."

The gifts we receive from God, like our speech, our talents, etc., are all intended to be used to show him how thankful we are. It is by doing this instead of simply what we want to do that we stay out of trouble. We may still find ourselves confronted by trouble occasionally, like when the knucklehead two cells down hides his contraband in our cell, and we get the blame for it. But if we have practiced using our talents in the right way, we will find it easier to bear the brunt of these difficulties without going back to the old way, with violence and anger. Let's look at another paragraph.

> *Let us then rise, since the* Scripture *calls us, saying: "It is now the hour for us to rise from sleep;" and having opened our eyes to the deifying light, let us hear with awestruck ears what the divine voice, crying out daily, does admonish us, saying: "Today, if you shall hear his voice, harden not your hearts." And again: "*He

that has ears to hear let him hear what the Spirit says to the churches." And what does He say? – "Come, children, listen to me, I will teach you the fear of the Lord." "Run while you have the light of life, that the darkness of death does not overtake you."

When we were on the streets, doing the things that got us into trouble, it sure seemed like we were completely awake. What Benedict means here is that we were not awake to the reality of God, but we were kind of asleep to it, not even realizing God's presence. And because of that, we were asleep to ourselves as well. We may think we know ourselves more than anyone else, but the deeper we go, the more we will find new and interesting things about ourselves, some of it good, and some of it not so good. So we have to open our eyes to the "deifying light." Deifying light is light that will cleanse us. It cleanses us by showing us our failures, shortcomings, and weaknesses. All of our screw-ups. BUT... it doesn't stop there. That would be kind of cold just to show us all of our weaknesses and then stop there. The deifying light shows us with love that all of our weaknesses and shortcomings are OK, because wherever we fall short, He will fill in the rest. That same deifying light also shows us the way to healing the effects of our past failures.

He says that if we hear His voice today, that we should not harden our hearts. This is a quote from the Bible (Hebrews 3.15). It is read daily by the monks of the Church to remind them that they can hear the voice of God each day in the words of others, or in more subtle ways, like watching a bird fly, or water drip from a faucet. These may seem like a waste of time, but sometimes you can watch water dripping from a faucet and get all kinds of crazy, profound insights! Try it sometime. It also calms you down. He tells us not to harden our hearts, meaning don't ignore it or fail to see His voice for what it truly is.

Finally, Benedict tells us to run while we have the light. When we are in the darkness – and let's face it: we've all been there – the only way to get out is if we have some light guiding us. God is the light, and by following Benedict's advice, we will learn to discern the light and escape the darkness. Now, let's move on to the next paragraph.

> *And the Lord seeking* His *workman in the multitude of the people, to whom* He *proclaims these words, says again: "Who is the man that desires life and loves to see good days?"* I*f hearing this you answer, "*I *am he," God says to you: "*I*f you will have true and everlasting life, keep your tongue from evil, and your lips from speaking guile; turn away from evil and do good; seek after peace and pursue it." And when you shall have done these things, my eyes shall be upon you, and my ears unto your prayers. And before you shall call upon me* I *will say: "Behold,* I *am here."*

This is a beautiful passage about the relationship between God and His followers. Notice that He does not force anyone to follow Him. Rather, he calls out to us, asking who will follow. Notice also that simply accepting what God offers is not enough. He goes on to say what will be required. Now I don't know about you, but the list of requirements seems daunting. These things may be easy for some people, but it is very hard to change our old ways. In prison, this can be even more difficult because we may hang out with some friends who would laugh at this stuff. Well, you don't have to change overnight, and I think it would be nearly impossible to do so. Rather, these things come gradually, like being healed from a deep wound or illness. As much as we may not want to admit it, we are ill in certain ways, and as we heal, we become better, stronger people. Not the kind who can pick fights with anyone and win, but the kind who are so strong that we avoid the fights, not by running away from our problems, but by confronting them head-on and dealing with them.

Finally, note in the last line that Benedict says God will answer us before we call Him. Now that's what I call service! He knows our needs before we even ask (Matthew 6.32). We may not always get what we ask for, but we will get what we need.

Look at the next two paragraphs.

What, dearest brothers, can be sweeter to us than this voice of the Lord *inviting us?* See, *in* His *loving kindness, the* Lord *shows us the way of life.*

Therefore, having our loins girded with faith and the performance of good works, let us walk His *ways under the guidance of the* Gospel, *that we may be found worthy of seeing* Him *who has called us to* His *kingdom.*

When we have our "loins girded" with faith and good works, we are so full of faith and have done many things with a good heart, that we are practically clothed in it. And by maintaining obedience, we walk in His paths. The next paragraph is very short.

If we desire to dwell in the tabernacle of His *kingdom, we cannot reach it in any way, unless we run there by good deeds.*

When Benedict says "good deeds" he is referring to the things that we do with a clear conscience and a good heart. The deeds by themselves are not enough. We must do them through love (Galatians 5.6, James 2.22-4). Let's see the next two paragraphs.

But *let us ask the* Lord *with the* Prophet, *saying to* Him: "Lord, *who shall dwell in* Your *tabernacle, or who shall rest in your holy hill?"*

After this question, brothers, let us listen to the Lord *answering and showing us the way to this tabernacle, saying:* "He *that*

> *walks without blemish and works justice; he that speaks truth in his heart; who has not used deceit in his tongue, nor has he done evil to his neighbor, nor has he taken up a reproach against his neighbor,"*

This is a quote from the 24th Psalm, and we are again presented with another daunting list. I think we have all done at least some of the things in this list that we are instructed not to do. However, because we can be forgiven and change our ways, there is hope. Let's look at the next paragraph.

> *It is he who has brought to nothing the foul demon tempting him, casting him out of his heart with his temptation, and has taken his evil thoughts while they were yet weak and has dashed them against Christ;*

It can be overwhelmingly difficult, if not impossible, to have such a great control of our wants and desires. We cannot do it without help. In asking for help, we gain humility, and the result is the ability to overcome. With help, we can lay hold of our thoughts, and change the way we actually think. Meditative practice will help us with this, but we must have patience and humility. Let's look at the next paragraph.

> *It is he who fearing the Lord are not puffed up by their goodness of life, but believing that the actual good which is in them cannot be done by themselves, but by the Lord, they praise the Lord working in them, saying with the Prophet: "Not to us, O Lord, not to us; by to Your name give glory." Thus also the Apostle Paul had not taken to himself any credit for his preaching, saying: "By the grace of God, I am what I am." And again he said: "He that glories, let him glory in the Lord."*

One of the most difficult things about meditation is dealing with the feeling that we are failing at it, that we are not doing it right, and that it is not working. The work is not done by us, but rather happens with practice. We do the practice, which seems like it's not getting us anywhere, and then one day we realize that we are changing. I remember the exact time that realization came to me. I was walking the yard in prison, and I saw some people who used to annoy me. I realized that they no longer annoyed me, and that I had done nothing to consciously remove that feeling. It just happened. My spiritual maturity had started to take place, and it was quite exciting.

When I was a child, my mother used to draw my height on the back of one of our closet doors. Every few months, we would go in there and draw a new line. After a while, I began to see real progress in growing, even though I never noticed any difference from day to day while looking in the mirror. I hadn't done anything to grow other than eat! The change happened gradually, and it is like that with our spiritual growth as well. It just happens. Our part is to meditate, to do the practice. That is like eating for the soul. The growth happens almost without us noticing it.

The next paragraph quotes the seventh chapter in the Gospel according to Matthew.

> *Hence, the Lord also said in the Gospel: "He that hears these my words and does them, shall be likened to a wise man who built his house upon a rock; the floods came, the winds blew, and they beat upon that house, and it did not fall, for it was founded on a rock."*

We will find that our strength, our ability to weather life's storms, will grow as well. The things that used to bother us won't. The tragedies in life won't seem to be as daunting. Notice that he doesn't say the man with the house on the rock doesn't experience a storm. He does experience a storm, but he can go through it, because his foundation is stronger. Let's move on to the next paragraph.

> *The Lord fulfilling these words waits for us from day to day, that we respond to His holy admonitions by our works. Therefore, our lives are lengthened for the amendment of the misdeeds of our present life; as the Apostle says: "Do you not know that the patience of God leads you to penance?" For the good Lord says: "I do not desire the death of the sinner, but that he be converted and live."*

This is a quote from 1 Timothy 2.4. Every single day that we wake up from sleep, we should be thankful to have awakened. We are alive! Each day is truly a gift. We didn't earn it. We didn't buy it. And, we don't deserve it or "have it coming." We take it for granted, because we have consistently awakened every day for a number of years, and it seems like it will keep happening. But when you really think about it, some day you won't wake up. That will be it. We have a limited number of days here, and we are told to use them wisely. Benedict is telling us that we are given days so that we can change our evil ways, because that is ultimately what God wants for us. The next paragraph really sums up most of what the Prologue is saying.

> *Now, brothers, that we have asked the Lord who shall dwell in His tabernacle, we have heard the conditions for dwelling there; and if we fulfil the duties of tenants, we shall be heirs of the kingdom of heaven.*

Benedict is saying that it is clear what we must do. Just knowing about it, though, doesn't get it done. We have to actually do something. Benedict is going to outline his way of living for us, and in the next paragraph, he talks about how we prepare for it.

> *Our hearts and our bodies must, therefore, be ready to do battle under the biddings of holy obedience; and let us ask God that He supply by the help of His grace what is hardly possible for us to do by nature. And if, flying from the pains of hell, we desire to reach life everlasting, then, while there is yet time, and we are still in the flesh, and are able during the present life to fulfil all these things, we must hurry to do now what will profit us forever.*

Here we see that Benedict is very aware that there are things in this Rule that will seem "hardly possible." However, he does not simply say to quit, or skip those things. Rather, he says we must "ask God" to give us assistance. Sometimes, we might feel weak asking for help. However, the weak ones are those who are afraid to ask. By asking, we learn how to do something, and become a better person. Asking for help is a lot smarter than trying to do something on your own and messing it up. Finally, let's look at the last paragraph of the Prologue.

> *We are, therefore, about to begin a school of the Lord's service, in which we hope to introduce nothing harsh or burdensome. But even if, to correct vices or to preserve charity, sound reason dictates anything that turns out to be somewhat stringent, do not at once run in dismay from the way of salvation, the beginning of which cannot but be narrow. But as we advance in the religious life and faith, we shall run the way of God's commandments with expanded hearts and unspeakable sweetness of love; so that never departing from His guidance and persevering in the monastery in His doctrine till death, we may by patience share in the sufferings of Christ, and be found worthy to be coheirs with Him of His kingdom.*

Once again, we see that Benedict is aware of the "harshness" of some of the things in the Rule. But, he says, don't run from it. He says if we stick to it, our hearts will expand, and we will find it easier to do these things on our own. We will grow and become better at doing the right thing.

Again, we persevere, meaning we stick to it until the end, and in doing so, we may "share in the sufferings of Christ." This does not mean that your reward for doing all of this is going to be more pain and suffering. We are going to experience suffering whether we follow the Rule or not. By following the Rule, we will be able to do so patiently.

This is the conclusion of the Prologue to the Rule of Benedict. In short, we have learned that this seems to be a way of living that is, at times, difficult to follow, but that we grow by keeping with it, and we become stronger in many ways. We are given each day as a gift to make ourselves better people. Our growth, our progress along the way, is not something we actually do – it just happens if we keep with the program. It was our own actions that caused a lot of the problems in our lives, and by changing the way we act and react, we can make our lives better.

1

On the Kinds of Monks

Welcome to monkhood! If you are embarking on this journey, then in a sense you are a monk. The word "monk" comes from an ancient word meaning "alone." This is because monks often separate themselves from others so that they can dedicate themselves to God. Typically today, monks live in communities called monasteries. If you are living in a prison, then you live in a community much like a monastery. There may even be other monks there with you!

Benedictine monks originally took three vows: obedience, conversion, and stability. These are the vows that I have currently taken. Conversion comes from a Latin verb meaning "to turn." Conversion is a vow that we are particularly interested in here, because it is really about daily conversion, or becoming a better person each day. Meditation helps us achieve that goal, and the Rule of Benedict helps guide us. Let's look at this first chapter.

> *It is well known that there are four kinds of monks. The first kind is that of Cenobites, that is, the monastic, who live under a rule and an Abbot.*
>
> *The second kind is that of Anchorites, or Hermits, that is, of those who, no longer in the first fervor of their conversion, but taught by long monastic practice and the help of many brethren, have already learned to fight against the devil; and going forth from the rank of their brothers well trained for single combat in the desert, they are able, with the help of God, to cope single-handed without the help of others, against the vices of the flesh and evil thoughts.*

We can see here that Benedict has divided all monks into four different classifications. The first, he says, are the Cenobites. That word, Cenobite, comes from two different ancient Greek words that mean community and life. They live their lives in a community. If you are in prison, then in a sense you are a Cenobite!

The second kind he calls Anchorites or Hermits. These kind live alone. Notice, however, that they must first live as Cenobites. They become Hermits after a "long" probation. They learn from the others in the monastery, and then are able to fight alone. Personally, I am still battling all kinds of issues within myself, and I need all the help I can get! At the present time, I do not live in a community, but I belong to a community, and am able to communicate with others from my community. This is how we learn to fight the struggles within. Remember, learning from others is not a sign of weakness, but of strength!

> *But a third and most vile class of monks is that of Sarabaites, who have been tried by no rule under the hand of a master, as gold is tried in the furnace; but, soft as lead, and still keeping faith with the world by their works, they are known to lie to God by their tonsure. Living in two's and three's, or even singly, without a shepherd, enclosed, not in the Lord's sheepfold, but in their own, the gratification of their desires is law unto them; because what they choose to do they call holy, but what they dislike they hold to be unlawful.*

The third kind do not sound like the sort of people we want to hang out with. These guys are what we sometimes call "posers." They pretend they are "all that," but in reality they are just trying to posture, trying to convince people that they are something they're not.

Benedict mentions that they have not been tested "in the furnace." Gold can be tested in a hot furnace. We can be tested in the "furnace" when trouble starts to come, when bad things happen. Those things are the furnace for us, and how we react to them is the test. They are the "lessons of experience." Some people have "been there, done that," and others just haven't. We used to call these "youngsters," or "first-termers," because they hadn't seen what prison is like yet. They hadn't been through the riots, the shakedowns, the lockdowns... all of that. You can see them coming a mile away! It's OK to be a first-termer, but Benedict is saying don't act like you've been around when you haven't. You'll be found out as a fake.

He goes on to say that they make up their own rules. They may say they live by a code of honor, but they made up their own code to suit themselves! Anyone can do that! My dog lives by his own code. So does my cat. They are not the same code, and they are not at all like mine, either. Benedict is saying that they go by their own code because they can't cut it with anyone else's system. They have to use their own code, because they are so soft, they wouldn't last a minute when the action starts.

> *But the fourth class of monks is that called Gyrovagues or Landlopers, who keep going their whole life long from one province to another, staying three or four days at a time in different cells as guests. Always roving and never settled, they indulge their passions and the cravings of their appetite, and are in every way worse than the Sarabaites. It is better to pass all these over in silence than to speak of their most wretched life.*

The fourth kind are the Gyrovagues. Wow. Benedict dislikes this bunch so much, he doesn't even want to talk about it. That's pretty bad.

We've all known people who skip from idea to idea, following the latest thing as if it is going to change their lives. As soon as something new comes along, off they go to follow that! That's basically the Gyrovague. The word "Gyro" is a Greek word that basically means circle. These Gyrovagues seem to be constantly running in circles. They lack stability. They can never stick with something or stay in the same place.

In meditation, there are many who have started, and then they give up after a little while. Often, the reason they give up is because they say they can't do it. In a way, this is ridiculous. They are expecting some fantastic trumpet to suddenly blow in their mind, a bright light to appear, and some great guru to appear to them, telling them that they are now enlightened. Sorry to break it to you, but as the cops used to say to me, "Ain't gonna happen." Not in a day, not in a week, and not in a month. Maybe not in a lifetime. Like I said earlier, I've been doing this for about ten years, and it hasn't happened to me yet. The important thing is, I'm not expecting it to happen. I'm not expecting anything to "happen." The "trick" to meditation is just to do it. Just sit down and shut up! Get quiet. When the distractions start (and they always do), go back to the meditation. Don't get mad. Don't get frustrated, because these things happen to everyone. They are supposed to happen because of the way our brains work. We are learning to discipline our minds by changing the way our brain works. Eventually, you will notice that you have greater control over the distractions. But they will still be there. Stability in practice will get you there. This fourth kind of monk lacks that stability. So how do we continue. Check out the last paragraph of this chapter.

> *Therefore, passing these over, let us go on with the help of God to lay down a rule for that most valiant kind of monks, the Cenobites.*

The Cenobite is what we want to be. And the Rule of Benedict is going to show us how to do it.

Before we move on to the next chapter, I'd like to say a little something about meditation. When we meditate, we try to choose a consistent time of the day so that we can get in the habit of doing it daily. We should try to meditate twice a day, for about 20 minutes or so, but we may want to start out with a shorter time, like five or ten minutes. It's important to develop the habit. When you're a monk, it's all about the habit! (a little monk joke – the clothing a monk wears is sometimes called a "habit")

Additionally, we are going to want to get in a good, comfortable posture. If your legs do not feel comfortable when they are twisted like pretzels, then don't twist them like pretzels! If you do, your meditation will be full of distractions like, "My leg hurts!" It's best to get into a position where you know you can relax. However, you don't want to fall asleep. For that reason, you should avoid lying down if at all possible. A comfortable sitting position is probably best, with your hands resting in your lap (maybe one hand resting in the other, cupped).

Close your eyes. The next step is to use a mantra. A mantra is a word that helps focus your mind to help you get rid of the distractions. You may have heard people meditate by saying "Om." That is a mantra common in the Far East. Since we are practicing Christian meditation, our mantra should probably be Christ-based. However, you should avoid using a word that will put images in your mind. You don't want to be concentrating on any thing so you want something that does not bring up any images. The World Community for Christian Meditation recommends using the mantra "Maranatha." This is a word found in the Bible (at the very end of 1 Corinthians). It is an Aramaic word, which is the language that Christ spoke. It means "Come, Lord." The best part about it is, you are probably not a fluent Aramaic speaker, so it is a good Mantra because you won't really be thinking of anything when you say it. If you are a fluent Aramaic speaker, then you might want to choose a different mantra.

When we begin to meditate, we close our eyes, sit with a straight back in a relaxed position, relaxed but still alert, and we begin saying the mantra to ourselves (not out loud). We say each syllable separately, like this, "Ma – Ra – Na – Tha." The "a" vowels here are pronounced like in the word "father." Kind of like when you stick your tongue out for the doctor, and say, "Ah."

Try meditating for five minutes the first time. If you have a timer with a gentle alarm, you may want to use that, or maybe a wristwatch with a beeper alarm on it.

The more you practice, the better you will feel. Just don't expect the trumpets and the guru to appear. And don't expect a drastic change in a short time. It takes practice.

2

What Kind of Man the Abbot Ought to Be

This chapter is somewhat lengthy, so I will break it down by paragraph, much like I did the prologue.

> *The Abbot who is worthy to be over a monastery, should always be mindful of what he is called, and make his works worthy of his name of Superior. For he is believed to hold the place of Christ in the monastery, when he is called by his name, according to the saying of the Apostle: "You have received the spirit of adoption of sons, whereby we cry Abba (Father)."*

The name Abbot comes from the Hebrew word for father, Abba. The Abbot of a monastery is like the warden of the prison. He is the main guy in charge of all the monks. He says what goes. So, in a sense, he is like a father of a large family. Benedict takes it a little further and says that the Abbot holds the place of Christ in the monastery. The quoted verse is speaking of adoption into a family, so that the title of father is appropriate.

I happen to know a little about this first-hand. I was adopted as a child. I have since reunited with my birth mother. However, my adoptive mother is still my mother, because she raised me. And my adoptive father is still my father, because he raised me. Benedict is saying that the Bible says we are adopted as sons, and that's why we can call God our Father. In the same respect, the authority in the monastery is from the Abbot, who exercises the authority with the guidance of the Holy Spirit, and therefore he is referred to as father, or Abbot.

> *Therefore, the Abbot should never teach, prescribe, or command (which God forbid) anything contrary to the laws of the Lord; but his commands and teaching should be instilled like a leaven of divine justice worked into the minds of his disciples.*

As we see in the following paragraph, the Abbot must lead based on divine principles, and never against anything Biblical. As you can see, the Abbot has some serious responsibility. There's even more.

> *Let the Abbot always bear in mind that he must give an account in the dread judgment of God of both his own teaching and of the obedience of his disciples. And let the Abbot know that whatever lack of profit the master of the house shall find in the sheep, will be laid to the blame of the shepherd. On the other hand he will be blameless, if he gave all a shepherd's care to his restless and unruly flock, and took all pains to correct their corrupt manners; so that their shepherd, acquitted at the Lord's judgment seat, may say to the Lord with the Prophet: "I have not hid Thy justice within my heart. I have declared Thy truth and Thy salvation." "But they despised and rejected me." Then at length eternal death will be the crushing doom of the rebellious sheep under his charge.*

The next paragraph seems to lay even more responsibility on the Abbot. As it turns out, if he makes a mistake and teaches them incorrectly, he bears the responsibility for that error, as well as all of the errors that are caused by his teaching. In other words, if the Abbot believes it is OK for the monks to get drunk on whiskey, then if one of the monks does this and as a result commits a horrible act under the influence, the Abbot is the one who has to pay for it! I don't mean pay as in money, but as in eternity! The Abbot is responsible for any teaching that causes a sin in any one of the brothers (the other monks in the monastery are called "brothers"). The only way he can get out of it is if he honestly taught them well, and they still refused to listen to him. Then, he's not responsible.

You may think all monks are well behaved, but that is not always the case. Benedict's own monks tried to poison him! Twice! Now that's an unruly bunch of monks!

> *When, therefore, anyone takes the name of Abbot he should govern his disciples by a twofold teaching; namely, he should show them all that is good and holy by his deeds more than by his words; explain the commandments of God to intelligent disciples by words, but show the divine precepts to the dull and simple by his works.*

I broke the following paragraph into two parts. In the first part, Benedict says that it is best to not only lead by telling people what is right, but also to lead by example. We've all known people who say one thing but do another. We sometimes call them "two-faced" because they are acting like they have two faces, two different people in one. Benedict is saying that the Abbot should teach both ways, by words and by example, because he says some of the monks learn more easily one way than the other.

You might say, "What does this have to do with me? I'm not an Abbot." That's a very good question. When I first read this section, I thought deeply about it, and what I got from it is that we all want to be leaders, but sometimes we are not prepared for the responsibility that goes along with leadership. I don't know about you, but being held accountable for everything I say and do is really serious accountability, and I am not sure I would want that. Personally, I don't think I am ready for that. I may never be ready for it. But because I have read this passage by Benedict, I understand better what some of those responsibilities are.

Additionally, I believe that each one of us will be called some day to take on some kind of leadership role. Benedict helps us understand the responsibilities of that role, and how seriously we need to take it. Let's look at the second half of this paragraph.

> *And let him show by his actions, that whatever he teaches his disciples as being contrary to the law of God must not be done, "lest perhaps when he hath preached to others, he himself should become a castaway," and he himself committing sin, God one day say to him: "Why do you declare My justices, and take My covenant in your mouth? But you have hated discipline, and have cast My words behind you." And: "You who saw the speck in your brother's eye, have not seen the beam in your own."*

Benedict is telling us that actions speak louder than words. He is saying that preaching the right thing and doing the wrong thing will bring judgment upon the Abbot, because he is leading by a bad example. The last part talks about finding fault in others when we have bigger faults ourselves. In other words, I have no place to talk about the sins of others when I am such a great sinner myself. Let's move on.

> *Let him make no distinction of persons in the monastery. Let him not love one more than another, unless it be one whom he finds more exemplary in good works and obedience. Let not one who was born into a wealthy family be preferred to a one who is a freed slave, unless there is some other reasonable cause. But if from a just reason the Abbot decides it is proper to make such a distinction, he may do so in regard to the rank of anyone; otherwise let everyone keep his own place; for whether bond or free, we are all one in Christ, and we all bear an equal burden of service under one Lord, "for there is no respect of persons with*

> *God." We are distinguished with Him in this respect alone, if we are found to excel others in good works and in humility. Therefore, let him have equal love for all, and impose a uniform discipline for all according to merit.*

We all have either seen favoritism or been directly involved in it one way or another. I have seen it in families, in jobs, and especially among friends. Here, Benedict is saying that the Abbot is not to play favorites. "Equal love" is what it's all about. And equal discipline as well. Just like the Abbot, we are not to play favorites with anyone. We can have friends, of course, and we can enjoy being with them more than others. What Benedict is speaking of here is favoritism in other ways. For example, let's say you're working in a shop and one of the tools is missing. Everyone gets searched for the missing tool except the guy who cleans the boss's desk. That's not fair! That's exactly what Benedict is saying. You have to be fair. Let's move on.

> *For in his teaching the Abbot should always observe that principle of the Apostle in which he says: "Reprove, entreat, rebuke," that is, mingling gentleness with severity, as the occasion may call for, let him show the severity of the master and the loving affection of a father. He must sternly rebuke the undisciplined and restless; but he must exhort the obedient, meek, and patient to advance in virtue. But we charge him to rebuke and punish the negligent and haughty.*

Something I never really appreciated until I went to prison was the vast diversity found in people. People are very different from each other. When we are in prison, we have to live in very close quarters with others twenty-four hours a day, seven days a week. We really get to know them. We learn their habits, both good and bad, as well as their mannerisms, etc. No wonder there is so much violence in prison! When people have to live that close together, they are bound to get on each other's nerves!

Because people are so different, Benedict says that the Abbot has to work with each person individually, in whatever way works best for them. When I was in school, the other kids used to make fun of me because they thought I was mentally retarded. In fact, I was very distracted by things going on in my head, and I had to learn to control and harness those things so that I could concentrate on what was going on. I needed a different approach to teaching. Not everyone can understand mathematics very well, but we might know how to adjust a carburetor. I, on the other hand, am fairly good at mathematics, but my knowledge of carburetors does not extend beyond how to spell the word. I really could not adjust one.

Benedict is saying that some people can learn simply by telling them something. Others need to be shown. In a monastery, there is often quite a bit of discipline to make sure that the monks keep in line. In the monastery of our hearts, it is no different. Some things you can tell me, and I have no problem understanding. Yet, much as I tried and wanted to stop, I could not stop drinking alcohol. Telling me about it did no good. It wasn't until the harshness of the law brought me to compliance that I was able to stop. People are different, and different people learn different things differently! Let's take a look at the next paragraph.

Let him not shut his eyes to the sins of evil-doers; but on their first appearance let him do his utmost to cut them out from the root at once, mindful of the fate of Heli, *the priest of* Silo. *The well-disposed and those of good understanding, let him correct at the first and second admonition only with words; but let him chastise the wicked and the hard of heart, and the proud and disobedient at the very first offense with stripes and other bodily punishments, knowing that it is written: "The fool is not corrected*

> *with words." And again: "Strike your son with the rod, and you shall deliver his soul from death."*

OK, you might be thinking to yourself, "Wow. This dude is serious!" Indeed, he was. Thankfully, the monasteries really don't beat the monks these days. If they did, I suspect there would be a lot fewer monks!

As I mentioned before, sometimes certain faults need severe correction before they can be stopped. Addiction is one example. We should look at this metaphorically, and think about some of the faults we have. We may say, "I don't know why, but every time I go back to the streets on parole, I always screw up." Perhaps we are being too soft on ourselves. Perhaps we really need to dig in and find out what is causing us to screw up every time we get out. Meditation can really help in diving into the past and uncovering some things that we might not want to deal with at first, but we'll be much happier and healthier once we have dealt with them.

Just a note about the example that Benedict gives us. He mentions someone named "Heli" at a place called "Silo." The translation we have of the Rule of Benedict here is based on an English translation of an older form of the Bible, probably from the Latin text called the Vulgate. I don't really want to get into technical details, but suffice it to say that in our more modern Bibles, "Heli" is actually "Eli" and "Silo" is "Shiloh." It all has to do with the way names are transliterated from one language to another. If you have the Douay-Rheims Bible, you will see the older spellings there as well. The passage relates to the first book of Samuel, the first chapter (1 Samuel 1).

> *The Abbot ought always to remember what he is and what he is called, and to know that to whom much has been entrusted,*

from him much will be required; and let him understand what a difficult and arduous task he assumes in governing souls and accommodating himself to a variety of characters. Let him so adjust and adapt himself to everyone – to one gentleness of speech, to another by reproofs, and to still another by entreaties, to each one according to his character and understanding – that he not only suffer no loss in his flock, but may rejoice in the increase of a worthy flock.

In this next paragraph, we are really going over the same points again. The Abbot has a tough job, and we see that Benedict says of him "much will be required." It almost sounds as if Benedict is trying to convince people that they really don't want the job! Indeed, that may be his intention in a way, because there is a lot of responsibility, and if the job falls into the wrong hands, disaster can strike.

In ourselves, it is the same way. Who is really ruling our lives? If the wrong guy is in control, we can really end up in some bad situations. We need to understand the importance of that job, and Benedict makes that clear here. Let's look at the next two paragraphs.

Above all things, that the Abbot may not neglect or undervalue the welfare of the souls entrusted to him, let him not have too great a concern about fleeting, earthly, perishable things; but let him always consider that he has undertaken the government of souls, of which he must give an account.

And that he may not perhaps complain of the desire of earthly things, let him remember what is written: "Seek first the kingdom of God and His justice, and all these things shall be added unto you." And again: "There is no desire to them that fear Him."

Benedict is saying that the matters of the world are of little consequence when compared to the state of the souls in his charge. I am reminded of the story of Benedict when there was a great famine in the land. All the wheat in the monastery was used up. There were only five loaves of bread remaining, and the monks were rather concerned about running out of food. Benedict saw this and told them, "Why are you sad about running out of bread? Today you are in want, but tomorrow you will have plenty." The following day 200 sacks of grain appeared at the gates of the monastery! Benedict knew that God would provide for the monks, as long has he provided for their souls.

Our concern, too, should be for our souls, and not as much for our food. Don't get me wrong: I think we still need to have jobs and work for food. It's all about priorities. For example, if you were on parole and starving, and someone offered you some money to sell some stolen articles, what would you do? It would be stupid to jeopardize your freedom (physically and spiritually) by selling the stolen items. If you starve to death, you die with a clean conscience and a clean spiritual record. And because of your honesty and integrity, God may provide you with some food. Let's look at the next paragraph.

> *And let him know that he who undertakes the government of souls must prepare himself to give an account for them; and whatever the number of brothers he has under his charge, let him be sure that on judgment day he will, without doubt, have to give an account to the* Lord *for all these souls, in addition to that of his own.*

Again, the Abbot is accountable for the souls in his care, and we are likewise accountable for our actions and thoughts. We should be warned here that if we profess to be some kind of spiritual teacher or preacher, then we put ourselves in this category, and if we teach incorrectly, whether due to our own ignorance or not, we are accountable for that teaching. If it leads one person astray, we are accountable for that soul. Thus, great care should be taken when teaching or taking on any kind of spiritual leadership role. Great care should also be taken when putting ourselves under the guidance of a teacher or master. We need to make sure that we are getting good guidance. And now, the last paragraph of Chapter Two.

> *And thus, while he is in constant fear of the Shepherd's future examination about the sheep entrusted to him, and is watchful of his account for others, he is made cautious also regarding his own account; and while by his admonitions he had administered correction to others, he is freed from his own failings.*

The last sentence here can be restated in the form of an often-cited quote: the teacher is the student, and the student is the teacher. The teacher learns a lot by working with the students, and thus the student becomes something of a teacher to the teacher. Anyone who has ever been in a position to teach others knows that, if they were open to receive it, they probably learned a lot from the experience. Note that the Abbot is not perfect, and we never need seek the perfect trainer. Even Socrates was found to be the wisest man simply because he thought he wasn't. It was his admission of not being wise that made him open to learning, which made him wiser.

Years ago, I was searching for the right church for me, or "steeple-chasing" as I called it. I was always frustrated that I couldn't find a church with people who adhered to what they taught. I was looking for the perfect church! What I failed to realize was, had I found the perfect church, it would no longer be perfect as soon as I joined it! Our spiritual teachers, be they individuals, church organizations, or books, will never be perfect, and we should not treat them that way. Nor should we ever think that we have all the answers, because it is at precisely that moment that we stop learning.

3

On Calling the Brothers for Counsel

Whenever weighty matters are to be done in the monastery, let the Abbot call together the whole community, and make known the matter which is to be considered. Having heard the brothers' views, let him weigh the matter with himself and do what he thinks best. It is for this reason, however, we said that all should be called for counsel, because the Lord often reveals to the younger what is best. Let the brothers, however, give their advice with humble submission, and let them not presume stubbornly to defend what seems right to them, for it must depend rather on the Abbot's will, so that all obey him in what he considers best. But as it is right for disciples to obey their master, so also it is right for the master to dispose all things with prudence and justice. Therefore, let all follow the Rule as their guide in everything, and let no one rashly depart from it.

Let no one in the monastery follow his own heart's wishes, and let no one dare to argue offensively with his Abbot, either inside or outside the monastery. If any one dares to do so, let him be placed under the correction of the Rule. Let the Abbot himself, however, do everything in the fear of the Lord and out of reverence for the Rule, knowing that, beyond a doubt, he will have to give an account to God, the most just Judge, for all his rulings. If, however, matters of less importance, having to do with the welfare of the monastery, are to be considered, let him use the counsel of the Seniors only, as it is written: "Do all things with counsel, and you shall not regret it when you have done it."

This is a very interesting chapter. Up to this point, we have seen the Abbot has a general authority in the monastery, and likewise we see that our spiritual master, whatever or whoever it may be, is given authority in our hearts. Here, it seems that the Abbot is being told to listen to the monks. Actually, Benedict is saying that the Abbot should listen to what the monks have to say before making any major decisions. Why? Because the Abbot cannot understand what all of the monks are thinking. One or more of the monks may know something about an aspect of the plan that the Abbot had not considered. It is with great humility that an Abbot does this, in essence making it known that he does not think he "knows it all," but rather that he is interested in what the monks have to say, because they may know the situation better.

As an example, I am reminded of a training session I had at work one day several years ago. I used to work in a telephone call center. The customers would call us when they had problems, and they were paying a lot of money to be allowed to call us. Well, the upper management ("the suits") had brought in someone who was supposed to teach us how to relieve stress, because the call center jobs would burn people out very quickly. This person basically told us that if we are stressed out when the phone rang, we shouldn't answer it. We were a call center! Answering the phone was our job! We tried to explain this to the person giving the training session, but he was unwilling to listen because "he was the expert."

Finally, my supervisor stood up and said, "If any of you don't answer the phone, you will be more stressed, because you'll be looking for another job!"

The problem was, upper management did not understand what we were doing "down in the ranks." It would have been smarter to ask us about the situation instead of telling us not to do our jobs.

No human being can keep the whole picture of a complex entity like a corporation or a monastery all in their head at once. That's why corporate bosses hire managers for different aspects.

When we are dealing with a problem, it is often very useful to get a fuller picture from those involved before trying to solve the problem ourselves. We may not understand the complete picture.

4

What the Instruments of Good Works Are

In this chapter, we have a list of 72 "instruments of good works." They are as follows:

1. In the first place to love the Lord God with the whole heart, the whole soul, the whole strength...
2. Then, one's neighbor as one's self
3. Then, not to kill...
4. Not to commit adultery...
5. Not to steal...
6. Not to covet.
7. Not to bear false witness.
8. To honor all men.
9. And what one would not have done to himself, not to do to another.
10. To deny one's self in order to follow Christ
11. To chastise the body.
12. Not to be attached to pleasures.
13. To love fasting.
14. To relieve the poor.
15. To clothe the naked...
16. To visit the sick.
17. To bury the dead.
18. To help in trouble.
19. To console the sorrowing.
20. To hold one's self separate from worldly ways.
21. To prefer nothing to the love of Christ.
22. Not to give way to anger.
23. Not to foster a desire for revenge.

24. Not to entertain deceit in the heart.
25. Not to make a false peace.
26. Not to forsake charity.
27. Not to swear, lest perchance one swear falsely.
28. To speak the truth with heart and tongue.
29. Not to return evil for evil.
30. To do no injury to anyone, and to patiently bear the injury done us.
31. To love one's enemies.
32. Not to curse them that curse us, but rather to bless them.
33. To bear persecution for justice sake.
34. Not to be proud...
35. Not to be addicted to wine.
36. Not to be a great eater.
37. Not to be drowsy.
38. Not to be lazy.
39. Not to be a murmurer.
40. Not to be a slanderer.
41. To put one's trust in God.
42. To refer what good one sees in himself, not to self, but to God.
43. But as to any evil in himself, let him be convinced that it is his own and charge it to himself.
44. To fear the day of judgment.
45. To be in dread of hell.
46. To desire eternal life with all spiritual longing.
47. To keep death before one's eyes daily.
48. To keep a constant watch over the actions of our life.
49. To hold as certain that God sees us everywhere.
50. To dash at once against Christ the evil thoughts which rise in one's heart.
51. And to disclose them to our spiritual father.
52. To guard one's tongue against bad and wicked speech.
53. Not to love much speaking.
54. Not to speak useless words and such as provoke laughter.

55. Not to love much or boisterous laughter.
56. To listen willingly to holy reading.
57. To apply one's self often to prayer.
58. To confess one's past sins to God daily in prayer with sighs and tears, and to amend them for the future.
59. Not to fulfil the desires of the flesh.
60. To hate one's own will.
61. To obey the commands of the Abbot in all things, even though he himself (which Heaven forbid) act otherwise, mindful of that teaching of the Lord: "What they say, do; what they do, do not do."
62. Not to desire to be called holy before one is; but to be holy first, that one may be truly so called.
63. To fulfil daily the commandments of God by works.
64. To love chastity.
65. To hate no one.
66. Not to be jealous; not to entertain envy.
67. Not to love strife.
68. Not to love pride.
69. To honor the elderly.
70. To love the younger ones.
71. To pray for one's enemies in the love of Christ.
72. To make peace with an adversary before the setting of the sun.
73. And never to despair of God's mercy.

Following this list are two paragraphs:

> *Behold, these are the instruments of the spiritual craft, which, if they have been applied without ceasing day and night and approved on judgment day, will win for us from the Lord that reward which He has promised: "The eye has not seen, nor the ear heard, neither has it entered into the heart of man, what things God has prepared for them that love Him."*

But the workshop in which we perform all these works with diligence is the enclosure of the monastery, and stability in the community.

What a list! Thankfully, most of the items on this list are common-sense. There are a few, however, that need some further explaining. I begin each explanation with the number of the item.

1 & 2: In Matthew 22.34-40, a lawyer has decided to see if he can trick Jesus by asking him what the greatest commandment is. The lawyer is probably expecting Jesus to answer with one of the ten commandments (Exodus 20). However, Jesus did not reply with one of them, but rather two other commands, the same as those listed in 1 & 2 above. When Jesus mentions these two, he says that the second one is like the first, and here's why: it is impossible to love God without loving your neighbor, and it is likewise impossible to love your neighbor without loving God. The reason is because whatever we do to the least, we do unto Him.

3-7: These are from the list of the ten commandments.

9: This is, in essence, identical to the "Golden Rule." This is why it is important for us to learn how to love ourselves and respect ourselves. Without loving ourselves, we cannot love others.

10: This says that we are to deny ourselves. This does not mean to deny our existence, as in saying something like, "I do not exist." That would be silly. What this means is that, when following a spiritual path, we may have to give up some things that we like, or we may have to do some things that make us feel uncomfortable. That's called "growing." Many children cry their first day of school because they do not want to be separated from their mothers. It is very uncomfortable. But look at all the benefits of an education! And soon afterward, the child is no longer sad going to school. We, too, will possibly have uncomfortable moments, but this is how we become better people.

11: When I read this, my mind first conjures images from the dark ages of monks flogging themselves with whips, and torturing themselves. If this were the case, I can assure you that the ranks of the monks would be much fewer than they are! Rather, chastising the body is practicing self-control. For example, I am an eater (see number 36). I love food. When I first went to jail before going to prison, I weighed 250 pounds (and I am not a very tall person!). In five months of jail, I lost 50 pounds (mostly because the food was so horrible!). I have learned that there are times when enjoying a little extra food is OK, especially on Thanksgiving. But most of the time, if I am eating too much, then I am wasting food and losing self-control in the process. By practicing self-control, we help not just our bodies but our minds as well. This is exactly the kind of self-discipline that helps us when meditating.

12: This simple command, the detachment from pleasures, is the aim of many Eastern beliefs. It is believed by Buddhists that all suffering stems from attachments, and that the only way to end suffering is to end attachments. Think of an attachment like an addiction – it's something you just can't do without (as if you're attached to it). Having the occasional pleasure is OK, but needing that pleasure can become problematic. Detachment leads to simplicity, and simplicity leads to peace.

20: Becoming a stranger to the ways of the world does not mean living in a fantasy separate from reality. If you take a wide-angle look at the world around you, it can be quite depressing. It seems like everyone is out to get his piece of the pie, and everyone is taking advantage of everyone else. That is the world Benedict is speaking of when he suggests becoming a stranger to the ways of the world. Become a stranger to taking advantage of others. Become a stranger to all the hurt, and ignoring the needs of others.

31: Loving our enemies is probably the most difficult biblical command of all. The very definition of "enemy" seems to lack all hint of love. How can I possibly go up to my enemy and say, "Hey dude, I love you." I'd probably get punched in the face! But loving an enemy does not mean you have to interact with them. There are people I have known who have acted against me like enemies. I can hope that they find happiness and enlightenment, but I don't have to be around them, especially if that would present a further danger to me.

34: There is a big difference between pride and self-confidence. We should have self-confidence, but not boast about how wonderful we are. That would be pride, and as the Old Testament says, "Pride goes before destruction, and a haughty spirit before a fall" (Proverbs 16.18). Many people quote this passage as, "Pride goes before a fall," but that is not what it says. It says it goes before "destruction." Ouch.

44: This is akin to the old Biblical phrase, "the fear of the Lord." It doesn't necessarily mean what we commonly think of as fear in this day and age. Rather, it means something more like a healthy respect. I respect the Lord, because he is all-powerful, etc., and he commands respect. There is an element of "what will happen if I don't" kind of thinking going on, but I don't constantly walk around in fear of what God is going to do to me. If that were the case, I'd be neurotic within a few days, or as we used to say, "fifty-one, fifty." To constantly live in fear is not healthy. However, we should have a general respect for authorities. Romans 13.1 says, "Let every soul be subject unto the higher powers. For there is no power but of God: the powers that be are ordained of God." In other words, anyone who is in a position of authority has been placed in that position by God. I know it may not seem true sometimes. We all know guards who are arrogant and sometimes act like jerks. But, according to the Bible, they were placed in that position by God. Maybe they are there to help us learn more humility! Well, in this case, Benedict is telling us that we should have the greatest respect for God.

47: This means to always be mindful of how fragile our lives are, and to know that at any moment our time may be up. If you're in a prison where there is a lot of violence, you probably already know this. I spent most of my prison time on relatively quiet yards. However, there were a lot of people with health problems, and a constant reminder of the fragility of life was the regularly occurring deaths. For a time, I worked in the office doing the paperwork each day on the new intakes and the deaths. It could be quite depressing to see the computer printout read "DECEASED" next to a name that I knew. However, it was balanced by the joy of almost daily seeing the word, "PAROLE" next to other friends' names. In a way, those who had died had paroled, too.

51: Disclosing your "evil thoughts" to another can seem like a very uncomfortable thing to do. I mean, would you talk to a "holy man" about the thoughts you are having for an old girlfriend? However, if you are fortunate to have a spiritual advisor (maybe even a chaplain), they can often help you through these difficulties. You may think that these people don't know what it's like to struggle with sexual desires, drug habits, etc. You would be surprised to find out how many of them have used drugs in their past, or been involved in illicit relationships. They may be living different lives now, but in no way have their lives been completely innocent. For example, I am a Benedictine oblate now, but I served ten years in prison for a crime I committed. I understand some of those issues. I've been addicted. I've been in situations of which I am not proud. However, I know that God will allow me to use that knowledge to help others. And a spiritual advisor can help you as well.

If you do not have a spiritual advisor, that's OK. However, I have found that it can really help to have someone on the path with you. Like I said earlier, a chaplain might be the perfect choice. Or, perhaps there is a relative you talk with regularly on the phone.

53-54: It has been said that it is better to be silent and thought a fool by others than to open one's mouth and prove the others right. As always, there is a time for talking, and Benedict is not saying that everyone should take a vow of silence. After all, God gave us tongues to use! We are meant to communicate that way. However, it seems that some people just love to hear themselves talk. They can be very annoying, and quite often their talking gets them into trouble. Don't be one of them.

61: Being called "Holy" is a good thing if you actually are holy. What Benedict is saying here is that it is better to be holy than not. If people call you holy and you're not, then you're just posing as something you're not.

69-70: There will always be someone in authority above us, and someone below us. We should have respect for the "seniors" or those who are either above us in authority or have "been around" longer. The "O.G.s" as we used to call them, can be full of wisdom. Likewise, then we should respect the younger ones as well. We should not boast about being above them, or take joy in having someone below us. After all, we are below someone as well.

Finally, notice in the last paragraph that Benedict refers to the monastery as a workshop. It is not a place where people are perfect (just like prison!), but rather a place where people are working on themselves (also like prison!). Some are working harder than others, and they will see better results.

5

On Obedience

Here begins a small treaty on humility. Humility is one of the most important aspects of the monk, and the meditator as well. It is a difficult aspect to develop, and one with which I have personally struggled. Having humility does not mean letting others walk all over you. Humility is the opposite of pride. It means not being full of pride. I enjoy writing. However, I am not John Steinbeck, nor shall I ever be. He was a great writer. I can aspire to be as great, and that is OK. I can say that I believe I am a good writer, but to unrealistically elevate some aspect of myself above the truth would be pride. To say that I think I can write better than John Steinbeck or Upton Sinclair, or any of the great writers would be silly. I would be making a fool of myself. In humility, I say that I am not a great writer, but I enjoy writing and I like my writing, and more importantly, I hope that others like it and can gain something from it.

We also have to beware of false humility. That is the kind of humility where we like to hear praise from others, so we purposefully deprecate ourselves (put ourselves down) in order to hear others say the opposite. For example, if I said, "I don't really write that well," in hopes of hearing someone say, "Oh, I think you're a great writer," then I am being humble on false pretenses; I am not really practicing humility, but rather I am enjoying the praise of others.

Benedict has pictured for us a ladder of steps to humility. He calls them "degrees." Oddly, he names the first degree twice, and each time it is slightly different. At first, I thought this was a mistake, but then I realized that they were actually the same.

Before I get into this part, I wanted to tell you that, after naming the first degree of humility here, Benedict will then go off-topic for a while, and then will return to the subject of the degrees of humility. So, this is just something of a preface on the subject. Let's look at what he says in the first two paragraphs.

> *The first degree of humility is obedience without delay. This graces those who, on account of the holy subjection which they have promised, or of the fear of hell, or the glory of life everlasting, hold nothing dearer than Christ. As soon as anything has been commanded by the Superior they permit no delay in the execution, as if the matter had been commanded by God Himself. Of these the Lord says: "At the hearing of the ear he has obeyed Me." And again He says to the teachers: "He that hears you hears Me."*
>
> *Such as these, therefore, instantly quitting their own work and giving up their own will, with hands disengaged, and leaving unfinished what they were doing, follow up, with the ready step of obedience, the work of command with deeds; and thus, as if in the same moment, both matters – the master's command and the disciple's finished work – are, in the swiftness of the fear of God, speedily finished together, the desire of advancing to eternal life urging them. They, therefore, seize upon the narrow way of which the Lord says: "Narrow is the way which leads to life," so that, not living according to their own desires and pleasures but walking according to the judgment and will of another, they live in monasteries, and desire an Abbot to be over them. Such as these truly live up to the maxim of the Lord in which He says: "I came not to do My own will, but the will of Him that sent Me."*

Here, Benedict has named the first degree of humility as "obedience without delay." When we have spiritual masters, we obey immediately. The same is true of the Divine Master. There are times when we know the right thing to do, but the longer we think about it, the more likely we are to do the wrong thing. That is why Benedict is saying to do it without delay. Do the right thing before you have a chance to convince yourself otherwise!

In meditation, this has a special meaning as well. We are told that, as soon as we become aware of the interruptions in our minds, the moments when we have started to think about the "worries of this world," we are to return to the mantra. Don't think, "I'm just going to stop for a moment, write this down, and then come back to meditation." Immediately come back to the mantra. Let the thought drift away and return to Christ-centeredness. The more you think about it, the longer you are "off center."

I want you to note also that Benedict speaks here of the "fear of God" again. This happens to be how he states the first degree of humility again in a later section. We'll come back to that when we get there. For now, let's look at the last paragraph for this chapter.

> *This obedience, however, will be acceptable to God and agreeable to men then only if what is commanded is done without hesitation, delay, lukewarmness, grumbling or complaint, because the obedience which is rendered to Superiors is rendered to God. For He Himself has said: "He that hears you hears Me." And it must be rendered by the disciples with a good will, "for the Lord loves a cheerful giver." For if the disciple obeys with an ill will, and grumbles, not only with lips but also in his heart, even though he fulfills the command, yet it will not be acceptable to God, who regards the heart of the murmurer. And for such an action he gains no reward; rather he incurs the penalty of murmurers, unless he makes satisfactory amendment.*

We see that those who harbor ill will in their giving are not credited with giving. I think of Cain, who sacrificed to God just like Abel, except that God did not find Cain's sacrifice acceptable. Perhaps Cain was complaining too much! Benedict is saying that if your heart is not in it, you may as well not do it.

There are days when I sit to meditate, and it just doesn't work. I just can't get into it. Maybe I'm "in a funk," but I just can't seem to quiet down. I have found, at least for me, that it's better to come back to it later. Maybe I can skip the morning session and come back to it in the evening. Otherwise, I just get more frustrated that things aren't "working." I always have distractions, and that's OK, but sometimes I just can't seem to keep coming back to the mantra. After giving it a serious try, that's when perhaps I need to center other parts of my life, and then find that meditating will help me center the rest.

The next chapter will be the "diversion" from the degrees of humility I spoke of, and then we will come back to the degrees after that.

6

On the Spirit of Silence

Silence is an important aspect in meditation. I speak not just of not making noise. That is silence, but there are other kinds of silence as well. Silence also means being still, and that has to do with the whole body, the whole mind, and the spirit. That is what is meant by the spirit of silence.

> *Let us do what the Prophet says: "I said, I will take heed of my ways, that I sin not with my tongue: I have set a guard to my mouth, I was unable to speak, and was humbled, and kept silence even from good things." Here the prophet shows that, if at times we ought to refrain from useful speech for the sake of silence, how much more ought we to abstain from evil words on account of the punishment due to sin.*

In the first paragraph, we see that Benedict is speaking of words, but this is only the literal sense. Indeed, we should keep our speech pure, and notice that there may be times when, even if we have something good to say, it might be best to say nothing. Proverbs 13.3 says, "He that keepeth his mouth keepeth his life: but he that openeth wide his lips shall have destruction." And Proverbs 21.23 says, "Whoso keepeth his mouth and his tongue keepeth his soul from troubles." So it seems that Benedict is saying that things will tend to go better for us if we don't talk unless we have to.

We should also keep a watch on our thoughts. Our minds can follow down some dangerous roads sometimes, and I'm sure we've all been in one of those situations. Sometimes it's just better not to think about some things. Let's look at the next paragraph.

> *Therefore, because of the importance of silence, let permission to speak be seldom given to perfect disciples even for good and holy and edifying discourse, for it is written: "In much talk you shall not escape sin." And elsewhere: "Death and life are in the power of the tongue."*

In the old monasteries, monks often took vows of silence, and they had to have permission to speak. As a matter of fact, some of the earliest forms of sign language were invented by monks so that they could communicate without talking. Thankfully, we don't have to take vows of silence in our daily lives, and especially in prison. But can you imagine, just for a moment, what prison would be like if no one spoke? Imagine how quiet the yard would be. Imagine how quiet the block would be. That would be something, wouldn't it? If everyone were doing it voluntarily, there would be a certain peace there, a peace that normally is missing. I used to meditate during the count times because the block was so quiet at those times. The peace is overwhelming if you stop to think about it. You might ask, what good would it do if everyone was quiet? Benedict talks a little about that in the following paragraph.

> *For it belongs to the master to speak and to teach; it is the job of the disciple to be silent and to listen. If, therefore, anything must be asked of the Superior, let it be asked with all humility and respectful submission.*

Benedict says that the disciple's part is to be silent and to listen. Again, we come back to that first word of the Rule of St. Benedict: listen. We learn not by speaking but by listening. We grow by listening. Not just listening with our ears, but with our hearts as well. After meditating, I often ask myself what my heart is feeling. What is my body trying to tell me? What is my heart and my mind trying to tell me? Sometimes, during meditation, certain experiences from the past may come up, and they come up for a reason. They may be very disturbing, but if they come up, then they are blocking me from going further, and they need to be addressed. We have to listen to ourselves, as well as to God. That's how we receive guidance in our lives, by listening.

> *But coarse jests, and idle words or speech provoking laughter, we condemn everywhere to eternal exclusion; and for such speech we do not permit the disciple to open his lips.*

In the last paragraph of this chapter, it sounds a little like Benedict is a killjoy or a "party pooper." What he's saying is that there is a time and a place for these things, and during meditation or prayer, that is not the time. I have occasionally had reason to laugh because something came to mind during meditation that was quite funny, maybe something I did years ago that now looks funny. That's OK, but I need to return to my meditation. I am thankful for the joyful times that these memories give me, but meditation time is for meditation, and so we quickly return to the mantra.

It is important to understand the necessity of silence in meditation, both in terms of lack of sound as well as keeping ourselves still in body and mind. Without this relaxation, we cannot be open to listen, and thus grow. We may not hear anything, but it is in the practice of keeping silent and still that growth comes.

7

On Humility

Perhaps my greatest lesson, and one I shall probably have to battle with until my death, is humility. It can be so difficult to be humble at times. It may be easy for some people to act humble, but to do so without feelings of anger or indignation can be much more difficult.

This chapter is one of the longest in the Rule, and it has been one of the most influential for me. It is a great formula for developing humility. Benedict breaks the chapter into steps, like on a ladder. However, they are not steps that are necessarily designed to be sequential. In other words, these are not accomplishments to be completed resulting in an official "I am now humble" proclamation. Rather, all these steps should really be worked on simultaneously. None of them is a prerequisite for the others, so none of them needs to be worked on before the others. They are all necessary, and all seemingly simple, yet amazingly difficult.

Benedict begins with an introduction to the steps in two paragraphs.

> *Brethren, the Holy Scripture cries to us saying: "Every one that exalts himself shall be humbled; and he that humbles himself shall be exalted." Since, therefore, it says this, it shows us that every exaltation is a kind of pride. The Prophet declares that he guards himself against this, saying: "Lord, my heart is not puffed up; nor are my eyes haughty. Neither have I walked in great matters nor in wonderful things above me." What then? "If I was not humbly minded, but exalted my soul; as a child*

that is weaned is towards his mother so shall You reward my soul."

Hence, brethren, if we wish to reach the greatest height of humility, and speedily to arrive at that heavenly exaltation to which ascent is made in the present life by humility, then, mounting by our actions, we must erect the ladder which appeared to Jacob in his dream, by means of which angels were shown to him ascending and descending. Without a doubt, we understand this ascending and descending to be nothing else but that we descend by pride and ascend by humility. The erected ladder, however, is our life in the present world, which, if the heart is humble, is lifted up by the Lord to heaven. For we say that our body and our soul are the two sides of this ladder; and into these sides the divine calling has inserted various degrees of humility or discipline which we must mount.

Benedict has painted a wonderful picture of a ladder. It seems rather awkward to us that one would ascend, or climb, by humility. Humility is normally seen as "lowering" ourselves. And again, he says we descend by "self-exaltation" which is normally seen as raising ourselves. Indeed, it is often in spiritual matters that what we think is the right way is, in fact, the wrong way. "There is a way which seemeth right unto a man, but the end thereof are the ways of death." (Proverbs 14.12)

So, Benedict has explained that the way up is humility and the way down is self-exaltation. In other words, the first shall be last, and the last shall be first, or as it says in Matthew 19.30, "But many that are first shall be last; and the last shall be first." Thus, we want to learn humility.

Benedict continues by mentioning the twelve steps or "degrees" of humility. He takes a bit longer with the first, covering seven paragraphs. Let's look at all of those together.

The first degree of humility, then, is that a man always have the fear of God before his eyes, shunning all forgetfulness and that he be ever mindful of all that God has commanded, that he always consider in his mind how those who despise God will burn in hell for their sins, and that life everlasting is prepared for those who fear God. And while he guards himself evermore against sin and vices of thought, word, deed, and self-will, let him also hasten to cut off the desires of the flesh.

Let a man consider that God always sees him from Heaven, that the eye of God beholds his works everywhere, and that the angels report them to Him every hour. The Prophet tells us this when he shows God thus ever present in our thoughts, saying: "The searcher of hearts and reins is God." And again: "The Lord knows the thoughts of men." And he says: "You have understood my thoughts from afar." And: "The thoughts of man shall give praise to You."

Therefore, in order that he may always be on his guard against evil thoughts, let the humble brother always say in his heart: "Then I shall be spotless before Him, if I shall keep myself from iniquity."

We are thus forbidden to do our own will, since the Scripture says to us: "And turn away from your evil will." And thus, too, we ask God in prayer that His will may be done in us. We are, therefore, rightly taught not to do our own will, when we guard against what Scripture says: "There are ways that to men seem right, the end of which plunges us into the depths of hell." And also when we are filled with dread at what is said of the negligent: "They are corrupted and become abominable in their pleasure."

But as regards desires of the flesh, let us believe that God is thus ever present to us, since the Prophet says to the Lord: "Before You is all my desire."

We must, therefore, guard against evil desires, because death has his station near the entrance of pleasure. For this reason, the Scripture commands, saying: "Go not after your lusts."

> *If, therefore, the eyes of the Lord observe the good and the bad and the Lord always looks down from heaven on the children of men, to see whether there is anyone that understands or seeks God; and if our actions are reported to the Lord day and night by the angels who are appointed to watch over us daily, we must ever be on our guard, brothers, as the Prophet says in the psalm, that God may at no time see us "going aside to evil and becoming unprofitable," and having spared us in the present time, because He is kind and waits for us to be changed for the better, say to us in the future: "These things you have done and I was silent."*

Benedict mentions that the first degree of humility is to keep the fear of God ever before our eyes and never forget it. What exactly is the fear of God? Does it mean that we are afraid of God? No, God is love, and we should not fear love, nor should we fear our Father who created each one of us and loves us individually. Rather, it is speaking of fear in the sense of respect. We should have a respect for God, just like our earthly fathers, because of our love for them. It is out of this respect and this love that we are obedient. Punishment may be a deterrent, but if you are in prison you know very well that the thought of going to prison is hardly a deterrent until the punishment happens. A better deterrent against sin is love and respect for God. It is out of this love and respect that we realize we are not God, we are not in charge of our own lives, and that realization helps develop humility. We begin to rely on God instead of ourselves. We begin to realize that our best plans may never happen if God decides to do something different. Thus, we are not in the driver's seat.

When you were a child, your parents may have had one of those little play steering wheels that would strap to your car seat, and you could pretend to drive just like mom or dad. Well, that is a little like our lives. We may think we are in charge because we have a steering wheel, but ultimately, we are not steering the car. God is.

The second degree of humility is, when a man loves not his own will, nor is pleased to fulfill his own desires but by his deeds carries our that word of the Lord which says: "I came not to do My own will but the will of Him that sent Me." It is likewise said: "Self-will has its punishment, but necessity wins the crown."

Quite often, doing what we want lands us in trouble. That is certainly how I ended up in prison, and I know it's how a lot of people end up in prison or worse. Our way is not always the right way. Careful and prayerful thought and consideration should accompany our actions to ensure that we are not doing something that is going to get us into trouble, either temporally or after this life.

The third degree of humility is, that for the love of God a man subject himself to a Superior in all obedience, imitating the Lord, of whom the Apostle says: "He became obedient unto death."

This one can be a little confusing at times. What if we have a boss who is corrupt and wants us to do something that we know is wrong? Is Benedict saying that we have to submit to what that guy says? Not necessarily. Note that the word "Superior" is capitalized here. That's the way it is in the translation I am using. Superior can mean someone here, like a boss, but I think Benedict is using it to mean a spiritual advisor, or someone we may use as a model for our lives. It's kind of like asking, "What would Jesus do?" when we do something. This helps us think more deeply about our actions. After all, isn't Jesus your Superior?

The next three paragraphs cover the fourth degree.

The fourth degree of humility is, that, if hard and distasteful things are commanded, even though injuries are inflicted, he accept them with patience with a silent mind, and not grow weary or give up, but hold out, as the Scripture says: "He that shall persevere to the end shall be saved." And again: "Let your heart take courage, and wait for the Lord."

And showing that a faithful man ought even to bear every disagreeable thing for the Lord, it says in the person of the suffering: "For Your sake we suffer death all the day long; we are counted as sheep for the slaughter." And secure in the hope of the divine reward, they go on joyfully, saying: "But in all these things we overcome because of Him that has loved us." And likewise in another place the Scripture says: "You, O God, have proven us; You have tried us by fire as silver is tried; You have brought us into a net, You have laid afflictions on our back." And to show us that we ought to be under a Superior, it continues, saying: "You have set men over our heads."

And fulfilling the command of the Lord by patience also in adversities and injuries, when struck on the one cheek they turn the other; the robber of their coat they give their cloak also; and when forced to go one mile they go two; with the Apostle Paul they bear with false brothers and "bless those who curse them."

In essence, Benedict is here telling us that we need to persevere to the end, and endure whatever comes our way without complaint. Note that the first sentence mentions "patience with a silent mind." How do we get a silent mind? Through meditation. By meditating, our minds will become more clear, and we will see our way through sufferings. Maybe not all the time, but we will begin to notice that we are becoming more patient, and our resolve will strengthen as well. I can even recall being surprised once when I was still in prison and someone wanted to fight with me. The guy hit me and I was surprised to find that I was not angry with him because I realized that he was doing the only thing he knew to do in the situation. From his point of view, he had no choice!

> *The fifth degree of humility is, when one hides from his Abbot none of the evil thoughts which rise in his heart or the evils committed by him in secret, but humbly confesses them. Concerning this the Scripture exhorts us, saying: "Reveal your way to the Lord and trust in Him." And it says further: "Confess to the Lord, for He is good, for His mercy endures forever." And the Prophet likewise says: "I have acknowledged my sin to You and my injustice I have not concealed. I said I will confess against myself my injustice to the Lord; and You have forgiven the wickedness of my sins."*

If you are not Catholic, then I need to explain a little about confession. I hear people sometimes ask, "Why do you confess to a priest, when you only need to confess to God?" Aside from the theological reasons, I want to here concentrate on other benefits. Confessing our sins and our inner thoughts can really bring a sense of relief. It cleanses us in a special way. The ancient Greeks used to do something like this when they went to the theater. It was what they called "catharsis," a method of cleansing by expressing themselves. All their anger, murderous thoughts, and sins were expressed in their plays, so they had a chance to act them out without actually committing these crimes. It was their way of confessing. Verbally confessing does the same thing for us. It will be very difficult in the beginning if you've never confessed to someone, but you'll find that it really can make you feel better. Benedict knew the benefits of confession, and that's why it is listed here as the fifth degree of humility.

I need to mention something here about confession. Please do not confess something to someone that will make the situation worse. For example, if a wife or husband is not aware that you had an affair, it may not be prudent to mention it to them. It may cause more problems than it resolves. Confess it to someone you can trust. I personally recommend a priest. Note that you can even confess crimes to priests, and they are under oath not to reveal that information to anyone else.

> *The sixth degree of humility is, when a monk is content with the poorest and worst of everything, and in all that is enjoined him he holds himself as a bad and worthless workman, saying with the Prophet: "I am brought to nothing and I knew it not; I have become like a beast before You, and I am always with You."*

In a literal sense, the sixth degree of humility seems like quite a bad way of thinking. It certainly would do nothing to boost one's self-esteem! In a not-so-literal sense, however, we begin to understand that all of our talents, our good traits and our abilities to do things well, are given us by God. We may say, "I worked for years in school learning electrical engineering or chemistry, so it did not come from God." We must look deeper and understand that the very ability for us to learn came from Him. Even the ability for us to breathe and have life is God-given.

Closer to the literal sense, we can reflect on many of our sins, our bad deeds of the past, and begin to think that God might be angry with us for all of our mistakes. Thankfully, God forgives us and understands that we are only human. After all, He made us that way! But knowing that we sometimes make mistakes does not give us a license to commit sins. We must remain in that humility, accepting responsibility for our own mistakes, and remembering that it is by the will of God that we are even able to ask for forgiveness.

> *The seventh degree of humility is, when, not only with his tongue he declares, but also in his inmost soul believes, that he is the lowest and vilest of men, humbling himself and saying with the Prophet: "But I am a worm and no man, the reproach of men and the outcast of the people." "I have been exalted and humbled and confounded." And also: "It is good for me that You have humbled me, that I may learn Your commandments."*

The seventh degree is a little like the sixth, especially in the sense that it seems that we are really putting ourselves down here. Sometimes in prison, we begin to think that we have a lot of friends, and we are well liked, so we tend to forget who we are in the eyes of the public. The public had us put in prison because they may look down on us. We have become "the scorn of men and the outcast of the people" in a very real way. It helps to look at our ordeal as a good thing, as a way for us to grow and learn the right way to live our lives, and that is what the last sentence is all about: "It is good for me that You have humbled me, that I may learn Your commandments." I think most people in prison would not have stopped committing their crimes without having been caught and put in prison. As much as I don't want to admit it, I think that was true of me. We should be thankful for the opportunity to clear our heads and get things right.

> *The eighth degree of humility is, when a monk does nothing but what is sanctioned by the common rule of the monastery and the example of his elders.*

In the eighth degree, we see a general example of simply following rules. We quickly learn from our experience in the world that when we don't follow the rules, we get in trouble. Benedict goes even further with the monks in the monastery, telling them that even if something is not specifically declared as wrong, they are not to do it unless they are specifically told to do so. This is a way of taming our own wills. It causes us to think through each action before we do it. Premeditation is one of the traits that distinguish human behavior from animal behavior. Still, it is surprising how little practice we seem to have in it! The Buddhists might call it "being mindful." Think things through before you do them. It may help keep you out of trouble!

> *The ninth degree of humility is, when a monk withholds his tongue from speaking, and keeps silent, not speaking until he is asked; for the Scripture shows that "in a multitude of words there shall be no lack of sin;" and that "a man full of tongue is not stable in the earth."*

With the ninth degree we have covered this ground before, and now Benedict lists the quality of silence as one of the degrees of humility. Remember that silence means more than just not talking. It can include silence of the body (stillness) and silence of the mind. Meditation will help us achieve that. It allows us to have greater control of our thinking patterns, and gain stability in general.

> *The tenth degree of humility is, when a monk is not easily moved and quick for laughter, for it is written: "The fool exalts his voice in laughter."*

The tenth degree, too, covers a previously covered topic. Here, Benedict is a little more explicit, not saying that we are to be free of laughter, but that we be "not easily moved and quick for laughter." In other words, not looking for a joke in everything. Take life with some seriousness, and enjoy the laughable moments with laughter when appropriate.

> *The eleventh degree of humility is, that, when a monk speaks, he speak gently and without laughter, humbly and with gravity, with few and sensible words, and that he be not loud of voice, as it is written: "The wise man is known by the fewness of his words."*

As we grow in meditation, we become beings of peace, and it is reflected in our voice as well. The eleventh degree implies that just talking to others can bring them peace, both in the tone of our voices as well as in the choice of our words. And sometimes, not saying anything will convey more peace and meaning.

> *The twelfth degree of humility is, when a monk is not only humble of heart, but always lets it appear also in his whole exterior to all that see him; namely, at the Work of God, in the garden, on a journey, in the field, or wherever he may be, sitting, walking, or standing, let him always have his head bowed down, his eyes fixed on the ground, ever holding himself guilty of his sins, thinking that he is already standing before the dread judgment seat of God, and always saying to himself in his heart what the publican in the Gospel said, with his eyes fixed on the ground: "Lord, I am a sinner and not worthy to lift up my eyes to heaven;" and again with the Prophet: "I am bowed down and humbled exceedingly."*

We all know people who seem to walk in such a way that you can tell their personality. We have seen people who walk as if they are the shot caller, the head honcho. In the twelfth degree, Benedict is saying that we should not walk that way, because it conveys a sense of pride. Note that keeping your eyes to the ground constantly might very well be impractical – you may run into a utility pole! But walking with your eyes in the sky can be just as dangerous, and it can convey a sense of pride that may be inflated above reality.

Finally, a closing paragraph on this chapter:

> *Having, therefore, ascended all these degrees of humility, the monk will presently arrive at that love of God, which being perfect, casts out fear. In virtue of this love all things which at first he observed with fear, he will now begin to keep without any effort, and as it were, naturally by force of habit, no longer from the fear of hell, but from the love of Christ, from the very habit of good and the pleasure in virtue. May the Lord be pleased to manifest all this by His Holy Spirit in His laborer now cleansed from vice and sin.*

Growing in meditation will result in a deeper love for God. I mentioned earlier that the “fear of the Lord” is sometimes perceived as a real fear, as us being afraid of God. But God is our Father, and we should not fear him in that sense, but rather have a respect for him. That respect is born of a great love that makes us want to please Him. No longer are there rules to be followed, but opportunities to express our love for our Father. And when our love for Him has matured, it will be a love in humility with great respect for Him.

8

On the Divine Office During the Night

The Catholic Church, of which Benedict was a member, has a set of prayers to be said at different hours of the day. These prayers have traditionally been said by the monks in monasteries, and they are still said in monasteries today. Because the prayers are set in different tones using different sequences for different times of the year, it was believed during the times of the early church that these prayers would be too difficult for the average layperson to say. Simpler prayers were taught to the people so that they could keep themselves in a meditative form of prayer (the Rosary is an example of a simple meditative prayer). This prayer system that the monks used was called "The Divine Office" or "The Liturgy of the Hours." In the Eastern Orthodox churches, it is often called "The Horologion."

Today, it is available in local languages all over the world for the layperson to say. The prayers of the Divine Office are usually given titles relating to when they are said: Matins, Lauds, Prime, Terce, Sext, None, Vespers, and Compline. Matins is during the night, Lauds is at sunrise, Prime at the first hour of the day, Terce at the third hour, Sext at the sixth hour, None at the ninth hour, Vespers near the end of the day, and Compline before bed.

In the next few chapters Benedict begins to describe the method for reading these prayers during different times, different days of the week, and different seasons. It can be rather dry reading, and it is very difficult to glean any kind of meaning from these sections other than just regulatory statements.

Like the dryness of the desert, however, it may look empty and dead at first, but there is life hidden here amongst the brush and sand.

> *Making due allowance for circumstances, the brethren will rise during the winter season, that is, from the calends of* November *until* Easter, *at the eighth hour of the night; so that, having rested until a little after midnight, they may rise refreshed. The time, however, which remains over after the night office will be employed in study by those of the brethren who still have some parts of the psalms and the lessons to learn.*
>
> *But from* Easter *to the aforesaid calends, let the hour for celebrating the night office be so arranged, that after a very short interval, during which the brethren may go out for the necessities of nature, the morning office, which is to be said at the break of day, may follow presently.*

First, we may notice that the times of prayer are different for different seasons. The word "calends" originally meant the beginning of the month in the Roman calendar, and it is, in fact, the root from which we get the word "calendar." Thus, the "calends of November" is simply the first of November.

Note also that Benedict has made provision for study time. Times that we spend in prayer should be set times during the day, and the same goes for meditation. Our meditation should be done as close as possible to the same times every day. This helps us develop the habit of doing it, because when we don't see immediate results, it becomes very easy to make excuses or forget to meditate. Meditating at the same times each day will develop the habit so that it eventually becomes automatic, something that we "just do."

9

How Many Psalms Are to Be Said at the Night Office

Here is the dryness I spoke of earlier. This chapter lists the psalms to be said during the Night Office of the Divine Office.

> *During the winter season, having in the first place said the verse: "O Lord, open my lips, and my mouth shall declare Your praise," there is next to be said three times, "Glory be to the Father...." To this the third psalm and the Gloria are to be added. After this the 94th psalm with its antiphon is to be said or chanted. Let the Te Deum follow, and after that six psalms with antiphons. When these and the verse have been said, let the Abbot give the blessing. All being seated on the benches, let three lessons be read alternately by the brethren from the book on the reading stand, between which let three responsories be said. Let two of the responsories be said without the Gloria, but after the third lesson, let him who is chanting say the Gloria. When the cantor begins to sing it, let all rise at once from their seats in honor and reverence of the Blessed Trinity.*
>
> *Let the inspired books of both the Old and the New Testaments be read at the night offices, as also the commentaries of them which have been made by the most eminent orthodox and Catholic Fathers.*
>
> *After these three lessons with their responsories, let six other psalms follow, to be sung with Alleluia. After these let the lessons from the Apostle follow, to be said by heart, then the verse, the invocation of the litany, that is, "Lord, have mercy." And then let the night office come to an end.*

Yeah, that's a lot of regulation there. I'd like to make a few comments on what is written here, and then on the general spirit and how we can find something in here to apply to our lives.

First, note that the modern "brief" version of the Divine Office (sometimes called the "Breviary") is significantly shorter than the description here. The verse, "O Lord, open my lips..." begins each day's prayer, and is only said at that hour. The other hours begin with "O God, come to my assistance." Note also that the Psalms are numbered according to a more ancient numbering (which is still used in some of the Eastern Orthodox churches), so some of the Psalm numbers may be off. For example, in the modern Office, it is Psalm 95, and not 94, that is said at the opening. Same Psalm, but in different Bibles, the Psalms are numbered differently, so if you are actually going to follow these numbers, you must keep that in mind. The "Te Deum" is sometimes now called the "Ambrosian Hymn."

It is interesting to note the great emphasis on the recitation of the Psalms during the Divine Office. It has been said that the book of Psalms is like a prayer book. It shows us different forms of prayer. Reading through, you are bound to find a psalm or two that you can really relate to.

Though typically meditation is done with a mantra in order to still the mind, I often find it fulfilling to read a psalm afterward. Do not read a psalm before meditation, as that will give your mind one more thing to distract itself! It is better to experience the psalm with a clear head, after 20 minutes or so of meditation.

Note also that this particular set of prayers described in this section is for the night office. As I mentioned earlier, the monks say the Divine Office throughout the day, including at night time. Though it may not be practical for us to pause seven or eight times a day to say prayers, we can take a lesson from the regularity of the monks' prayers, and make sure to set aside a time for meditation and prayer each day.

10

How the Night Office Is to Be Said in the Summer Season

Benedict understood clearly the difference of the seasons, and makes provision here for the shortness of the nights during the summer months.

> *From Easter until the calends of November let the whole list of psalms, as explained above, be said, except that on account of the shortness of the nights, no lessons are read from the book; but instead of these three lessons, let one from the Old Testament be said from memory. Let a short responsory follow this, and let all the rest be performed as was said; namely, that never fewer than twelve psalms be said at the night office, exclusive of the third and the 94th psalm.*

Note that Benedict does not use the shortness of the nights to forego the lessons altogether, but rather he has shortened the lesson to allow for sleep. Likewise, when we are pressed for time and find that a 20 minute meditation is just not possible, we may consider a ten minute meditation instead of skipping the meditation altogether.

11

How the Night *Office* Is *to* Be *Said on Sundays*

Sundays are considered special days to Christians, and the prayers said in the Divine Office are a little more special on Sundays. After all, it is the day that we celebrate the resurrection of Jesus. For this reason, Benedict alters the typical office recitation to include quite a bit more content.

> *For the night office on Sunday the monks should rise earlier. At this office let the following regulations be observed, namely: after six psalms and the verse have been sung, as we arranged above, and all have been properly seated on the benches in their order, let four lessons with their responsories be read from the book, as we said above. In the fourth responsory only, let the Gloria be said by the chanter, and as soon as he begins it let all presently rise with reverence.*
>
> *After these lessons let six other psalms with antiphons and the verse follow in order as before. After these let there be said three canticles from the Prophets, selected by the Abbot, and chanted with Alleluia. When the verse also has been said and the Abbot has given the blessing, let four other lessons from the New Testament be read in the order above mentioned.*
>
> *But after the fourth responsory let the Abbot chant the hymn Te Deum. When this has been said, let the Abbot read the lesson from the Gospel, all standing with reverence and awe. When the Gospel has been read let all answer Amen, and immediately the Abbot will follow up with the hymn "To You be praise," and when he has given the blessing the Morning Office will begin.*

Let this order of the night office be observed on Sunday *the same way in all seasons, in summer as well as in winter, unless (which* God *forbid) the brethren should rise too late and part of the lessons or the responsories would have to be shortened.* Let *every precaution be taken that this does not occur.* I*f it should happen, let him through whose neglect it came about make due satisfaction for it to* God *in the oratory.*

12

How the Morning Office Is to Be Said

The Morning Office follows the Night Office. As you will see, it is very much like the Night Office, and uses numerous Psalms, as all the Offices do.

> *At the Morning Office on Sunday, let the 66th psalm be said first simply, without an antiphon. After that let the 50th psalm be said with Alleluia; after this let the 117th and the 62d be said; then the blessing and the praises, one lesson from the Apocalypse, said by heart, a responsory, the* Te Deum, *the verse and the canticle from the Gospel, the litany, and it is finished.*

The reference to the "Apocalypse" is to the book "Revelation" which in former editions was referred to as the Apocalypse.

I think it is interesting that Benedict has chosen Psalm 50 (which in most Bibles today is Psalm 51) to read in the morning. Psalm 51 includes the following lines (from the Douay-Rheims bible):

> *2 Wash me yet more from my iniquity, and cleanse me from my sin.*
> *3 For I know my iniquity, and my sin is always before me.*
> *4 To thee only have I sinned, and have done evil before thee: that thou mayst be justified in thy words and mayst overcome when thou art judged.*

There is a serious acknowledgement of our own sins here, and in Benedict's schedule, this takes place right at the beginning of the day. The first verse I cited, "Wash me yet more..." is also recited by the Catholic Priests during mass when they wash their hands symbolically before consecration of the Eucharist.

However, we are not just left to wallow in our sins. It goes on...

> *10 Create a clean heart in me, O God: and renew a right spirit within my bowels.*
> *11 Cast me not away from thy face; and take not thy holy spirit from me.*
> *12 Restore unto me the joy of thy salvation, and strengthen me with a perfect spirit.*

The text of the tenth verse should be a daily prayer for us all: Create a clean heart in me, O God! And this, the prayer for a clean heart, a renewed spirit, is why this particular Psalm is perfect for morning recitation. A clean heart and renewed spirit are the perfect way to begin each day.

13

How the Morning *Office* Is *to* Be *Said on* W*eekdays*

Traditionally, when the Divine Office was begun, monks were walking on their way to the room where they all pray together. One of the Psalms is usually chanted on the way, and at such tempo that it gives time for all to get to the oratory on time.

> *On week days let the* Morning *Office be celebrated in the following manner:* Let *the 66th psalm be said without an antiphon, drawing it out a little as on* Sunday, *that all may arriver for the 50th, which is to be said with an antiphon.* A*fter this let two other psalms be said according to custom; namely, the 5th and the 35th on the second day, the 42d and the 56th on the third day, the 63rd and the 64th on the fourth day, the* 87*th and the* 89*th on the fifth day, the 75th and the 91st on the sixth day, and on* Saturday *the* 142*d and the canticle of* Deuteronomy, *which should be divided into two sections, each ended with a* Gloria. *On the other days, however, let the canticle from the* Prophets, *each for its proper day, be said as the* Roman Church *sings it.* A*fter these let the psalms of praise follow; then one lesson from the* Apostle, *to be said from memory, the responsory, the* Te Deum, *the verse, the canticle from the* Gospel, *the litany, and it is finished.*

We can see here that the weekdays run in a cycle, with the same Psalms being recited on the same days of the week. The Divine Office runs on several cycles: there is an annual cycle of the seasons, a four-week cycle of the Psalter (i.e. how most Psalms are read), a weekly cycle as seen above, and a daily cycle in the recitation of the prayers at specific hours. One can see why the Divine Office is sometimes called "The Liturgy of the Hours."

In the last two paragraphs of the chapter, we see some interesting information about the Lord's Prayer.

> *Owing to the scandals which tend to spring up, the morning and the evening office should, plainly, never end unless the Lord's Prayer is said in the hearing of all by the Superior in its place at the end; so that in virtue of the promise which the brothers make when they say, "Forgive us as we forgive," they may cleanse themselves of failings of this kind.*
>
> *At the other hours which are to be said, however, let only the last part of this prayer be said aloud, so that all may answer, "But deliver us from evil."*

It was apparent to Benedict that the Lord's Prayer helped against scandal, problems with forgiveness, and delivery from evil. This is probably why he emphasized its importance. It is such a simple prayer, and memorized by so many from a young age, and yet it is this prayer with which Christ responded when asked how we should pray.

14

How the Night Office Is to Be Said on the Feasts of the Saints

In the Divine Office, the prayers of the "ordinary" (those prayers that are typically said in a cycle) are set aside on special holy days and feast days. On these special days, there are prayers specific to that day.

> *On the feasts of the saints and on all solemn festivals let the night office be performed as we said it should be done on Sunday; except that the psalms, the antiphons, and the lessons proper for that day should be said; but let the number of psalms mentioned above be maintained.*

The reason for this was to ensure that the lessons gleaned from reading the Psalms or the other readings were relevant to the celebration of the day. In the same manner, we may find that reflection following meditation may take on a more relevant light depending on the season or the day. We may find special significance on Thanksgiving, Christmas, Easter, or even our own birthday. These days are special to us, and as we mature spiritually we may find that their special meanings may change as well. They may also take on greater depth of meaning.

15

At What Times "Alleluia" Is to Be Said

This is, to me, one of the most interesting regulations in the Rule of St. Benedict. The reason I find it interesting is because, at first glance, it seemed to me to be so very petty. Yet, after reading the Divine Office for some time, I began to notice something. Let's look at the text first.

> *From holy Easter until Pentecost let the Alleluia be said without intermission, both with the psalms and with the responsories; but from Pentecost until the beginning of Lent let it be said every night at the Night Office with the six last psalms only. However, on all Sundays outside of Lent, let the canticles, Morning Office, Prime, Terce, Sext, and None be said with Alleluia. Let Vespers, however, be said with the antiphon; but let the responsories never be said with Alleluia, except from Easter to Pentecost.*

This might seem like just another regulation for the sake of regulation. When I started reading the Divine Office, I was still in prison, and I found it difficult at first to understand how to follow the book. I used a Breviary, and I eventually got the hang of it. After a while, I noticed that the lack of Alleluias during Lent made the prayers seem a little more somber and less joyful. Of course, this is exactly the intent! Lent is a time of remembrance of the sufferings of Christ, and their relation to our own sufferings here in this lifetime.

Additionally, during the Easter season, the Alleluias are doubled, meaning that where one would normally say, "Alleluia," instead you say, "Alleluia Alleluia." This highlights the joy of the risen Christ. Not only are the Alleluias back, but they are back twice as strong!

If you attend a Catholic Mass, you may notice a parallel. At the services in the United States during Lent, the Gloria ("Glory to God in the highest...") is not said. It returns on Easter Sunday.

16

How the Work of God Is to Be Performed During the Day

Recall that Benedict uses "the Work of God" as a synonym for the Divine Office. The shortest prayers in the Office are said during the day.

> *As the Prophet says: "Seven times a day I have given praise to You," this sacred sevenfold number will be fulfilled by us in this way if we perform the duties of our service at the time of the Morning Office, Prime, Terce, Sext, None, Vespers, and Compline; because it was of these day hours that he had said: "Seven times a day I have given praise to You." For the same Prophet said of the night watches: "At midnight I arose to confess to You."*
>
> *At these times, therefore, let us offer praise to our Creator "for the judgments of His justice;" namely, at the Morning Office, Prime, Terce, Sext, None, Vespers, and Compline; and let us rise at night to praise Him.*

The quote here is from Psalm 119.164, which reads in the Douay-Rheims version: "Seven times a day I have given praise to thee, for the judgments of thy justice." This quote is also mentioned in the introduction to the Breviary. In the more modern Breviaries, the prayers are renamed to make it a little easier: invitatory, morning, midmorning, midday, midafternoon, evening, night.

Many religious traditions use prayer throughout the day. Most monasteries today use just the morning and evening prayers.

17

How Many Psalms Are to Be Chanted at These Hours

As I mentioned earlier, the daytime prayers are some of the shortest in the Breviary, and that is made evident in this chapter.

> *We have now arranged the order of the psalmody for the night and the morning office; let us next arrange for the succeeding Hours.*
>
> *At the first Hour let three psalms be said separately, and not under one Gloria. Let the hymn for the same Hour be said after the verse "God, come to my assistance," before the psalms are begun. Then, after the completion of three psalms, let one lesson be said, a verse, the "Lord, have mercy," and the ending prayers.*
>
> *At the third, the sixth, and the ninth Hours, the prayer will be said in the same order; namely, the verse, the hymn proper to each Hour, the three psalms, the lesson, the verse, the "Lord, have mercy," and the ending prayers. If the brotherhood is large, let these Hours be sung with antiphons; but if small, let them be said without a break.*
>
> *Let the office of Vespers be ended with four psalms and antiphons; after these psalms a lesson is to be recited, next a responsory, the Te Deum, a verse, the canticle from the Gospel, the litany, the Lord's Prayer, and the ending prayers.*
>
> *Let Compline end with the saying of three psalms, which are to be said straight on without an antiphon, and after these the hymn for the same Hour, one lesson, the verse, "Lord, have mercy," the blessing, and the ending prayers.*

Again, we see a rather regimental formula for the reading of the Daily Office. Its main focus here is on the Psalms, which are one of the few changing elements of the prayers. Typically, each of the hours (i.e. morning, evening, etc.) is said in the same format. The morning prayers are different from the evening, but the morning always follows the same formula. The only real change from day to day is which Psalms are read. That is why Benedict is concentrating so much on the Psalms. Next, we will see in what order they are read.

18

In What Order the Psalms Are to Be Said

Similar to the previous chapter, this chapter concentrates on the psalms said during the daily prayers. While the previous chapter explained how many were said at each office, this chapter concentrates on specifically which psalms are to be read. There is a lot of text here, and it is fairly regimental. There is not much to be said, although there are a few points worth illustrating.

> *In the beginning let there be said the verse, "God, come to my assistance; Lord, make haste to help me," and the Gloria, followed by the hymn for each Hour.*

The opening verse in the U.S. version now reads, "O God, come to my assistance. O Lord, make haste to help me." While the opening to the morning office, "O Lord, open my lips..." is from Psalm 51, this passage, which is said at the opening of all the other offices, is from Psalm 70.1. The original text (in Hebrew) sounds more like an urgent plea than a prayer. It would more directly translate as something like "O God, deliver me! Hurry, O Lord, to help me!" I don't know about you, but there are times I have almost literally cried out like that!

> *At Prime on Sunday, then, there are to be said four sections of the 118th psalm. At the other Hours, however, namely Terce, Sext, and None, let three sections of the same psalm be said.*

Psalm 118 is only about 29 verses long. However, this is not the Psalm Benedict intends. Recall that I mentioned earlier about some versions of the Bible numbering the Psalms differently. The Psalm intended here is what we now know of as Psalm 119, which is enormously long. It is, in fact, the longest chapter in the Bible, at 176 verses! Reciting this Psalm in one of the offices would take quite a while, and Benedict understands that, so he has graciously suggested that it be read in sections. Some Bibles still have this Psalm divided into sections, and some do not. There are 22 sections, each named after a letter of the Hebrew alphabet (the verses in each section all start with that letter in the Hebrew original). Thus, verses 1–8 are the first section, 9–16 the second, and so on.

> *But at Prime on Monday let three psalms be said, namely, the first, the second, and the sixth; and the same each day at Prime until Sunday, let three psalms be said each time in consecutive order up to the 19th psalm, yet so that the ninth psalm and the 17th each will be divided into two with two Glorias; and thus it will come about that at the night office on Sundays we always begin with the 20th psalm.*

Here again we see that Benedict has divided some of the Psalms due to their length. Also, notice that he has arranged them so that they repeat on a weekly cycle. This is one of the cycles in the Divine Office.

> *At Terce, Sext, and None, on Monday, however, let the nine sections which remain over the 118th psalm be said, three sections at each of these Hours.*
>
> *The 118th psalm having in this way been parceled out for two days, namely, Sunday and Monday, let there be sung on Tuesday for Terce, Sext, and None, three psalms each, from the 119th to the 127th, that is, nine psalms. These psalms will always be*

> *repeated at the same Hours in just the same way until Sunday, observing also for all these days a regular succession of the hymns, the lessons, and the verses, so, namely, that on Sunday the beginning is always made with the 118th psalm.*

These two paragraphs cover the daytime hours of Terce, Sext, and None. Again, note the division of Psalm 118 and the preservation of the weekly cycle.

> *Let Vespers be sung daily with the singing of four psalms. Let these psalms begin with the 109th to the 147th, excepting those which are set aside for the other Hours; namely, from the 117th to the 127th, and the 133d, and the 142d. All the rest are to be said at Vespers; and as the psalms fall three short, those of the previously mentioned psalms which are found to be longer, are to be divided; namely, the 138th, the 143d, and the 144th. But because the 116th is short, let it be joined to the 115th.*

Psalm 116 in the other numbering system is what most of our Bibles will have as Psalm 117, the shortest chapter in the Bible: only two verses. For this reason, Benedict has suggested appending it to the previous Psalm, 116 (or 115 in the other numbering system).

> *The order of the psalms for Vespers having thus been arranged let the rest, namely, the lessons, the responsories, the hymns, the verses, and the canticles, be said as we have directed above.*

And that concludes Benedict's coverage of the Vespers, which are the evening prayer.

> *At Compline, however, let the same psalms be repeated every day; namely, the 4th, the 90th, and the 133rd.*

Like the day offices, Compline is relatively short and simple, and Benedict follows this simplicity by making the Psalm readings just as simple. In the modern Breviary, there are still different Psalms read each day of the week. Compline is the office usually prayed just before going to bed.

> *Having arranged the order of the office, let all the rest of the psalms which remain over, be divided equally into seven night offices, by so dividing such of them as are of greater length that twelve fall to each night.*

The Night Office is the last one listed. Benedict follows with a conclusion.

> *We especially stress this, that, if this distribution of the psalms should displease anyone, he arrange them if he thinks another way is better, by all means seeing to it that the whole Psalter of one hundred and fifty psalms be said every week, and that it always start again from the beginning at Matins on Sunday; because those monks show too lax a service in their devotion who in the course of a week chant less than the whole Psalter with its customary canticles; since we read, that our holy forefathers promptly fulfilled in one day what we lukewarm monks should, please God, perform at least in a week.*

After all the regulations on Psalms and which are to be said at which office, notice that Benedict now is basically saying, "Feel free to change it around if you like." He asks only that the entire book of Psalms is read in a week. That is still quite a task for someone with a busy schedule. I would like to emphasize that reading and praying the Psalms can be a wonderful experience, so if you are inclined to read the entire book of Psalms, I would like to suggest perhaps taking four weeks to complete it, as the current Divine Office Breviary has done. This is a much more reasonable schedule for someone who is not a monk in a monastery. We rarely get a break during our daily jobs to sit down and read a psalm. It might be nice to read some in the morning before getting out of bed, and some in the evening before going to bed. I would recommend reading a psalm or two after each meditation. The psalm is likely to reach a greater depth in us when our minds and spirits are centered.

19

On the Manner of Chanting the Psalms

While you may not specifically be praying the Divine Office each day, the advice Benedict offers here can be applied to prayer in general

> *We believe that God is present everywhere and that the eyes of the Lord behold the good and the bad in every place. Let us firmly believe this, especially when we take part in the Work of God. Let us, therefore, always be mindful of what the Prophet says, "Serve the Lord with fear." And again, "Sing wisely." And, "I will sing praise to You in the sight of the angels." Therefore, let us consider how it is good for us to behave in the sight of God and His angels, and let us so stand to sing, that our mind may be in harmony with our voice.*

Benedict here reminds us that when we pray we are in the presence of angels. Note that he says our mind should be "in harmony" with our voice. How often we recite via rote repetition some memorized prayers, and we are not even thinking consciously about what we are saying! Imagine going to your dad and asking for the keys to the car, but not even paying attention to what you're saying. He would notice! He would see that you don't really care about what you're saying, so why should he bother listening? Our Father in heaven wants us to really feel what we are saying to him, to have a genuine relationship with him, or to "be real" with Him. Otherwise, we're just being fake, and He can see right through it.

One of the benefits of daily meditation is a greater mindfulness. It doesn't happen instantly, but over time, the more we meditate, the more we become mindful of things and the easier it is to feel what we are saying when we pray. I noticed after meditating for a while that I actually became aware of the lyrics in some of my favorite songs. I had been listening to them for twenty years or so, and never even really paid attention to the words! When we are in prayer, we should be mindful of what we are saying, and when we are in meditation we should be watchful that, as soon as we become distracted, we return to our mantra. By doing so, we will exercise our ability to be mindful.

20

On Reverence at Prayer

Mindfulness during prayer can be enhanced when we are in a "reverent" mood, as Benedict explains in this chapter.

> *If we do not step out to approach men who are in power, except with humility and reverence, when we wish to ask a favor, how much must we appeal to the Lord God of all things with all humility and purity of devotion? And let us be assured that it is not in many words, but in the purity of heart and tears of compunction that we are heard. For this reason prayer ought to be short and pure, unless, perhaps it is lengthened by the inspiration of divine grace. At the community exercises, however, let the prayer always be short, and the sign having been given by the Superior, let all rise together.*

Christ Himself pointed out that there were those who made loud and lengthy prayers for the purpose of appearing pious among others. This is an effort to convince others that you are something you're not. It is a form of pride and lying. Recall the story in the Gospel about the two men praying in the synagogue (Luke 18.10-14):

> *Two men went up into the temple to pray: the one a Pharisee, and the other a publican. The Pharisee standing, prayed thus with himself: O God, I give thee thanks that I am not as the rest of men, extortioners, unjust, adulterers, as also is this publican. I fast twice in a week: I give tithes of all that I possess. And the publican, standing afar off, would not so much as lift up his eyes*

> *towards heaven; but struck his breast, saying: O god, be merciful to me a sinner.* I *say to you, this man went down into his house justified rather that the other: because every one that exalteth himself, shall be humbled: and he that humbleth himself, shall be exalted.*

The prayers of the more humble man were heard, and according to Jesus, he was justified. The other was not. We may have a lot to say, and we may have lengthy prayers for things we feel strongly about, but they should not be made in public in the sight of others. That is what Benedict is saying.

21

On the Deans of the Monastery

Monastic communities come in different sizes, just like companies, families, and prisons. Instead of creating a one-size-fits-all form for all communities, Benedict here describes a position that may be necessary in larger communities.

> *If the brotherhood is large, let brothers of good repute and holy life be chosen from among them and be appointed Deans; and let them take care of their deaneries in everything according to the commandments of God and the directions of their Abbot.*
>
> *Let such be chosen Deans as the Abbot may safely trust to share his burden. Let them not be chosen for their rank, but for the merit of their life and their wisdom and knowledge; and if any of them, puffed up with pride, should be found blameworthy and, after having been corrected once and again and even a third time, refuse to amend, let him be deposed, and one who is worthy be put in his place.*
>
> *We make the same regulation with reference to the Prior.*

An adage that has proven itself throughout time is, "Power corrupts." From people of high position like kings and presidents, to people of lower positions, human beings seem to let any kind of power go to their heads. They end up abusing the power to serve their own needs, often at the expense of others. Benedict was very aware of this very human tendency, and he takes precaution here to ensure that they either remain free of such corruptions, or that they are replaced if such corruption happens. He notes that they must observe the commandments of God and the instructions of the Abbot. They are to be chosen according to their wisdom and their worthiness. And finally, if they are found to let the position "go to their head," they are to be given three warnings, and then replaced.

In our daily lives, we often see people who let power go to their heads. They are sometimes in a position of authority above us, such as prison guards or supervisors at work. It can be difficult to deal with these people at times, but we must remember that they are giving us a great gift: humility. Saint Paul, in his letter to the Romans (Rom. 13.1 KJV), says, "Let every soul be subject unto the higher powers. For there is no power but of God: the powers that be are ordained of God." In other words, those who are in authority over us were placed in that position over us by God, and so we should be thankful for the lesson in humility it teaches us.

Additionally, Jesus tells his apostles not to exercise authority over others in the same corrupt way as others: "But Jesus calling them, saith to them: You know that they who seem to rule over the Gentiles, lord it over them: and their princes have power over them. But it is not so among you: but whosoever will be greater, shall be your minister." (Mark 10.42-43) So we must also remember this when we are placed in a position of authority over someone else.

22

How the Monks Are to Sleep

Never let it be said that the Rule fails to regulate any part of a monk's life, including how he or she sleeps! This may seem a little extreme, but there are reasons for having this rule in place.

> *Let the brothers sleep singly, each in a separate bed. Let them receive the bedding according to their mode of life, according to the direction of their Abbot. If it can be done, let all sleep in one room; but if the number does not allow it, let them sleep in groups of ten or twenty with the seniors who have charge of them.*
>
> *Let a light be kept burning constantly in the room until morning.*
>
> *Let them sleep clothed and girded with belts or cords, that they may be always ready; but let them not have knives at their sides while they sleep, lest they be wounded in their dreams; and the sign having been given, rising without delay, let them hasten to outpace each other to the Work of God, yet with all gravity and decorum.*
>
> *Let the younger brethren not have their beds beside each other, but intermingled with the older ones; and rising to the Work of God, let them gently encourage one another on account of the excuses of the drowsy.*

It may seem odd to have to state that each monk should sleep in a separate bed, as we might have difficulty imagining sharing a bed with someone (other than perhaps a spouse). But in Benedict's day, often resources were somewhat scarce, and it might have happened that certain monasteries allowed monks to share beds. This invites trouble, as any prison inmate knows! My last few years in prison, I was housed in a dormitory setting, and I cannot tell you how many times inmates were caught in the beds of other inmates during the night. Obviously, this sort of thing is to be avoided in a monastery, and so the rule has stated that they should all sleep in separate beds.

The term "bedding suitable to their manner of life" simply means that some places are colder than others, and some people may be more sensitive to the cold than others. Thus, sufficient bedding should be given to each monk.

The light burning is utilitarian, in the sense that people who have thoughts of breaking regulations often find the cover of dark helpful to disguise their actions. However, there is also the symbolic meaning, the Light of Christ, always with you, and never leaving one in the dark.

The monks were also to sleep in a state of preparedness. This was to ensure that they would be ready for the prayers when the bell rang to wake them. It is also a lesson to us in constant preparedness for the coming of our Lord. Even if he should come at night.

Note that Benedict does not allow the younger monks to sleep next to each other, but rather that they be interspersed among the older monks. Anyone who has raised more than one child knows that having two of them in the same vicinity at night only leads to trouble! They'll talk when they should be sleeping, etc. Thus, Benedict has the older monks placed between them to ensure a peaceful sleep for all.

And finally, Benedict knows that while some people can spring from the bed at the sound of a bell as if they were ejected by some hidden mechanism, others are quite lethargic at first, and are likely to need a little "encouraging."

Sleeping is a necessary thing: we all need it. However, the night time lends itself to the opportunities for quite a lot of evil. We need to be cautious and keep our own lights burning to make sure we are never left in the dark.

23

On Ex*communication for* F*aults*

Now we find what I am sure has been the much-anticipated section on "punishments." Contrary to popular opinion, monks today do not spend their day flogging themselves or purposefully wearing uncomfortable and incomprehensibly itchy clothing. At least not the ones I know. Although there is some mention of corporal punishment herein, it must be understood in context, both to the original author, and how we apply something like that to our lives today.

> *If a brother is found stubborn or disobedient or proud or murmuring, or opposed to anything in the Holy Rule and an arguer of the commandments of his Superiors, let him be admonished by his Superiors once and again in secret, according to the command of our Lord. If he does not amend let him be taken to task publicly before all. But if he does not reform even then, and he understands what a penalty it is, let him be placed under excommunication; but if even then he remains obstinate let him undergo corporal punishment.*

Upon reading this, we see that Benedict encourages discretion at first, confronting the disobedient monk in private regarding his behavior. If he continues, he is again confronted privately. If no change is made, he is then publicly admonished in the hopes that further embarrassment will convince him to change his ways. If not, the end results in excommunication.

In the modern sense, we think of excommunication as something like expulsion from the community. It's like being "kicked out" of the group. However, Benedict explains excommunication in more detail in the following chapter.

Personally, I am a firm believer in the use of both positive and negative reinforcement when it comes to teaching proper behavior. Benedict seems to use the same model. Many dwell on the negative aspects of the punishments in the Rule, but Benedict also rewards those who possess "worthiness of life" with appointments as dean or prior (though some who have served in such positions may differ as to whether this constitutes positive reinforcement!). The point I am making is that, in our daily lives, we are going to "mess things up" from time to time. We should not flog ourselves mentally, but work on our weaknesses, and be thankful for our strengths. God often blesses us with strengths that can be used to overcome our weaknesses.

24

What the Manner *of* Excommunication *Should* Be

Here, Benedict explains what he means by "excommunication."

> *The degree of excommunication or punishment ought to be measured out according to the gravity of the offense, and to determine that is left to the judgment of the Abbot.*
>
> *If, however, anyone of the brothers is found in smaller faults, let him be banned from eating at the common table. The following shall be the practice respecting one who is excluded from the common table: that he does not chant a psalm or an antiphon nor read a lesson in the oratory until he has made satisfaction; let him take his meal alone, after the meal of the brothers; thus: if, for instance, the brothers take their meal at the sixth hour that brother will take his at the ninth, and if the brothers take theirs at the ninth, he will take his in the evening, until by due satisfaction he obtains pardon.*

The general principle outlined here is one of exclusion. The offending brother is to be excluded from general fellowship because he has acted in a way that disturbs the fellowship of his brothers. In prison, we learn that we are excluded from society because we have violated the regulations of society, so it is much the same thing.

One may wonder why not intoning the Psalms and antiphons is considered a punishment. The intonation of Psalms is something done as a community, and Benedict means to make sure this person feels excluded from the community as much as is possible. This, of course, is the "excommunication" for "smaller faults."

We can look at this passage as carrying a deeper meaning as well. We may have certain behaviors that need to be "excommunicated" (or eradicated) from us so that we can rejoin society in a healthy, productive way. If we are already in society (i.e. not in prison), we may need to excommunicate certain behaviors to continue being a contributing member of society. Perhaps we have a tendency to use language that is not always (or sometimes rarely) appropriate. With practice, we can eliminate such actions. In some cases, like addictions, we may need to alter our thinking patterns, and excommunicate them from our minds. It takes practice.

In meditation, too, we excommunicate the distractions that come into our minds. This is a little different, because the distractions are not necessarily "bad," but they are simply distracting, and we are attempting to train our minds to focus and be more mindful. In order to achieve progress, we will need to have lots of practice excommunicating distractions. In a sense, distractions can be a good thing because the more distractions one has, the more practice one has in eradicating them!

25

On Graver Faults

Now, Benedict addresses the punishment for "bigger" or more serious problems.

> *But let the brother who is found guilty of a graver fault be excluded from both the table and the oratory. Let none of the brothers join his company or speak with him. Let him be alone at the work enjoined on him, persevering in penitential sorrow, mindful of the terrible sentence of the Apostle who said, that "such a man is delivered over for the destruction of the flesh, that the spirit may be saved in the day of the Lord." Let him get his food alone in such quantity and at such a time as the Abbot shall deem fit; and let him not be blessed by anyone passing by, nor the food that is given him.*

Ouch! This is of the same flavor as the previous chapter, but a little more bitter. This is a serious severing of contact from the brethren, and I can imagine that part of Benedict's reasoning here was to avoid someone in error drawing others into the same situation. In other words, keeping the problem isolated so that it doesn't spread. However, there is much punishment involved here as well, such as the monk not being blessed and his food not being blessed. In essence, a blessing would be wasted on someone who is defying the laws of God. For example, imagine asking God to bless a sin you are about to commit! While the person is not a sin, the person may be living in sin, and blessing them while they continue to be in defiance would be akin to casting pearls before swine. The monk needs to address the issue before expecting any further blessings. This is not to say that they cease to pray for the monk. On the contrary (as will be explained further in an upcoming chapter).

In our lives, we may have certain “bad monks” wandering around in our heads, and we need to understand that sinful actions or thoughts are not blessed by God. When we are not acting in accordance with his laws, we may be limiting our own potential.

26

On Those Who Without an Order From the Abbot Associate With the Excommunicated

Benedict has said that those guilty of serious offenses are not to associate with the other monks. As we all know, rules get broken, and Benedict outlines the punishment of breaking this rule, since it is designed to contain the fault and prevent its spread.

> *If any brother presumes to associate with an excommunicated brother in any way, or to speak with him, or to send him a message, without the command of the Abbot, let him incur the same penalty of excommunication.*

Benedict inflicts the same punishment of excommunication on a monk who associates with an excommunicated monk. First, the second monk has disobeyed the Abbot by associating with the punished monk. Second, it is possible that the first monk might have been attempting to justify his actions and gain solidarity with other monks. If this is the case, then the problem is much worse, and excommunication is warranted until satisfaction (which will be explained later) is made.

Ideas can be good or bad, and ideas spread. We as humans have an amazing ability to justify our actions, right or wrong, good or bad. We have to be on guard when we justify our actions that we are not justifying wrong or bad actions. It's difficult to be objective with ourselves, but objectivity is necessary to determine whether we are simply attempting to justify a bad action, or whether we are rightfully justified.

27

How Concerned the Abbot Should Be About the Excommunicated

As everyone knows, and as I have mentioned earlier, power corrupts. Because of this, when someone disobeys an Abbot, it is possible for the Abbot to take personal offense, and treat the disobedient monk in an overly harsh way. Benedict explains how the Abbot should treat the excommunicated monk.

> *Let the Abbot show all care and concern to avoid offending brothers because "they that are in health do not need a physician, but they that are sick." Therefore, like a prudent physician he ought to use every opportunity to send "senpectae," namely, discreet elderly brethren, to console the wavering brother, as it were, in secret, and induce him to make humble satisfaction; and let them cheer him up "lest he be swallowed up with too much sorrow;" but, as the same Apostle said, "confirm your charity towards him;" and let prayer be said for him by all.*
>
> *The Abbot must take the utmost pains, and strive with all prudence and zeal, that none of the flock entrusted to him perish. For the Abbot must know that he has taken upon himself the care of infirm souls, not a tyrannical rule over the strong; and let him fear the threat of the Prophet by whom the Lord says: "What you saw to be fat, you took to yourselves, and what was diseased you threw away." And let him follow the loving example of the Good Shepherd, who, leaving the ninety-nine sheep on the mountains, went to seek the one that had gone astray, on whose weakness He had such pity, that He was pleased to lay it on His sacred shoulders and thus carry it back to the fold.*

Benedict has used a word here that has caused a lot of controversy over the years. Just what exactly does he mean by "senpectae?" There are a couple of theories, and one of the most relevant in my opinion is that it is similar to the ancient word "sumpaictes" which basically means something like a group of elders. That seems to agree with his explanation as well. Sending in others, i.e. not the guy in authority, is a good idea. The Abbot knows they will "back him up" by agreeing with him, and he knows they will encourage the wayward monk because they are, after all, brothers. At least in the monastic sense. Sometimes, a little gentle encouragement from someone we know and respect is all that is necessary to help us.

Of course, the monks are encouraged to pray for their brother. By today's standards, prayer is often seen as a last resort. In fact, it should be the first resort. Praying for something may "consecrate" a subsequent action that will lead to success. Also, praying first shows God that you are putting Him in the driver's seat, placing Him first.

Benedict continues with the simile of a shepherd and his sheep. The Abbot should treat his monks like a shepherd, not abusing or hating any of them, but rather caring for their well-being. You may not have ever dealt with actual sheep, but when I was much younger I had a friend who had sheep. Trust me: they need leadership! Goats, on the other hand, are obstinate, and constantly want to go their own way and do their own thing. When Jesus spoke of the sheep and the goats in Matthew 25.32-46, it was not by accident that he chose to use those two animals as examples. Sheep will follow a leader. Goats will not unless forced to. Benedict would prefer that his Abbots treat his monks as sheep, in a caring and loving way, but also making sure that they do not stray (as sheep are apt to do).

Additionally, sheep are in need of gentle care. Thus, it is the role of an Abbot to care for his monks, and in that way to guide them. Yelling, screaming, and arguing are rarely effective ways of guiding someone. I recall a friend of mine in prison whose cell-mate was stealing his food at night. One night, he awoke to find his cell-mate in his locker. Rather than starting a fight or argument, he got up and turned on the light. His cell-mate was startled and not sure what to do. My friend calmly went to his locker, took out some food, and started sharing it with his cell-mate. They both ate in silence. Afterward, my friend said, "Next time you're hungry, just let me know. I'll be happy to share what I have with you." His cell-mate never stole food from him again. It was his gentleness that was much more effective in resolving the issue than a fight ever would have been.

28

On Those Who Do Not Amend After Repeated Corrections

Just like the goats, there are some people who will simply insist on doing their own thing, breaking rules, and generally being disorderly and disobedient. They occasionally find their way into a monastery, and Benedict has some guidance on how to deal with them as well.

If a brother has often been corrected and has even been excommunicated for a fault and does not amend, let a more severe correction be applied to him, namely, proceed against him with corporal punishment.

But if even then he does not reform, or puffed up with pride, should perhaps, which God forbid, even defend his actions, then let the Abbot act like a prudent physician. After he has applied soothing lotions, ointments of admonitions, medication of the Holy Scriptures, and if, as a last resource, he has employed the caustic of excommunication and the blows of the lash, and sees that even then his pains are of no avail, let him apply for that brother also what is more potent than all these measures: his own prayer and that of the brethren, that the Lord who is all-powerful may work a cure in that brother.

But if he is not healed even in this way, then finally let the Abbot dismiss him from the community, as the Apostle said: "Put away the evil one from among you;" and again: "If the faithless depart, let him depart;" lest one diseased sheep infect the whole flock.

This is perhaps the most difficult regulation in the Rule to apply to today. Again, we see the use of corporal punishment. We must understand first that this is no longer in use. Second, we can apply its severity in a metaphorical way to faults we find in ourselves. This would be akin to the passage in Matthew 5.29-30: "And if thy right eye scandalize thee, pluck it out and cast it from thee. For it is expedient for thee that one of thy members should perish, rather than that thy whole body be cast into hell. And if thy right hand scandalize thee, cut it off, and cast it from thee: for it is expedient for thee that one of thy members should perish, rather than that thy whole body be cast into hell." If we took this passage literally, there would be a lot of blind amputees in the world. When Jesus spoke these words, he was speaking about removing those things which may cause us to sin. Some may even argue that he was speaking of members in a congregation. Likewise, when someone is causing enough problems that the problems themselves may spread to others, then expulsion is the wise thing to do.

29

Whether Brethren Who Leave the Monastery Ought to Be Received Again

While many may see the Rule as harsh, there are certainly a lot of second chances for those who mess things up every once in a while.

> *If a brother, who through his own fault leaves the monastery or is expelled, desires to return, let him first promise full amendment of the fault for which he left; and thus let him be received in the last place, that by this means his humility may be tried. If he should leave again, let him be received even a third time, knowing that after this every means of return will be denied him.*

It almost seems like three chances at this are too many. But, Benedict is beneficent if nothing else. And so is God.

We have a tendency to ride the winds of doctrine and be tossed about like a boat on the sea. Paul said it best in Ephesians 4.14: "That henceforth we be no more children tossed to and fro, and carried about with every wind of doctrine by the wickedness of men, by cunning craftiness, by which they lie in wait to deceive." In other words, we change our minds a lot. We may decide that following God is a great idea. Two weeks later, we may decide that it's not for us. The following day, we may change our mind again.

I remember hearing one time that, in the sense of addictions, every time we falter, it makes staying "straight" much more difficult the next time. Thus, we need to really make an effort, if we are going to eradicate some harmful or wrong habits from our lives, to make sure we stick to it. One of the vows modern monks make is the vow of stability, which I discussed a little in the first chapter. That is what this chapter is talking about: stability. Stability doesn't mean always doing the same thing; it means always aiming to do the right thing without constantly changing our direction. It's an integral part of calming down and making still our bodies and our minds.

30

How Young Boys Are to Be Corrected

In the days of Benedict, it was somewhat common for parents to send their children to a monastery. It was rather like going to Catholic school today. If the practice had still been common when I was a child, I think it likely my parents would have sent me! Here, Benedict describes the different manner of discipline for the boys.

> *Every age and understanding should have its proper discipline. Whenever, therefore, boys or immature youths or such as can not understand how grave a penalty excommunication is, are guilty of a serious fault, let them undergo severe fasting or be disciplined with corporal punishment, that they may be corrected.*

Boys will be boys, and certainly Benedict understood that. They would find excommunication perhaps welcome in some cases, finally a time to be alone! Away from those stuffy old monks! So, Benedict, in his wisdom, believed that they needed a different incentive to behave. Remember that "corporal punishment" was the way most people disciplined their unruly children at the time. We can be thankful it is no longer the case.

We should understand from this that how a situation is handled should take into account specifics about the situation. The same goes for the people involved. Different measures for different situations, and different ways of handling different people. We are not all alike (thankfully), and our diversity is part of what makes us human beings. When we deal with others, either in sensitive situations or even in everyday conversation, we need to take into account the person and the situation.

When I was in prison, I remember a guy named Charlie who lived in the cell next to me for a while. Charlie was probably in his fifties or sixties and had some apparent developmental disabilities, and he tended to speak in a gruff voice and a harsh manner with many people. I think I might have been Charlie's only friend.

One day, Charlie said the wrong thing to a younger inmate who thought he needed to "prove" himself, and the guy stabbed Charlie. It was very sad. Because he was unable to identify the guy (although everyone else knew who had done it), Charlie was transferred to another prison (for his personal safety). I never saw him again. Certainly, the younger guy could have taken into account Charlie's situation and realized that it was just Charlie being Charlie.

Perhaps an argument we recently had with someone could have been avoided had we taken the time to listen to the other person and attempt to understand their situation.

31

What Kind of Man *the* Cellarer *of the* Monastery *Ought to* Be

Apart from being a somewhat difficult word to pronounce, the Cellarer is the person in the monastery responsible for the food and drink. He orders supplies as needed, and keeps an inventory of the food to make sure it is not being invaded by rodents or secretive, wayward monks. This chapter is somewhat lengthy, so I will discuss it one paragraph at a time.

> *Let there be chosen from the brotherhood as Cellarer of the monastery a wise man, of settled habits, temperate and frugal, not conceited, irritable, resentful, sluggish, or wasteful, but fearing God, who may be as a father to the whole brotherhood.*

All of the traits described in the first paragraph should be fairly obvious desirable traits for someone overseeing a food supply, especially that the cellarer should be "frugal" or not wasteful.

> *Let him have the charge of everything, let him do nothing without the command of the Abbot, let him do what has been ordered for him and not grieve the brothers. If a brother should request anything of him unreasonably let him not sadden the brother with a cold refusal, but politely and with humility refuse him who asked wrongly.*

The second paragraph describes traits that are certainly a good idea, though possibly not quite as obvious as those from the first. The section on not "grieving" is important to maintain a sense of peace in the community. Likewise, when someone has made an unreasonable demand on us, we should remember that they may not understand why the demand is unreasonable to us. Thus, we should "not grieve" but rather take the time to give the reason for the refusal.

> *Let him be watchful of his own soul, always mindful of the saying of the Apostle: "For they that have ministered well, shall gain for themselves a good status."*

The phrase "they that have ministered well" is basically referring to someone who has done a good job. Sometimes it seems like we work just to get a paycheck and hand it over to someone else (i.e. the rent, bills, etc.). We would be much happier if our work had some higher purpose. We should remember that when we work, we work for the Lord. St. Paul talks about this in Colossians 3.23: "Whatsoever you do, do it from the heart, as to the Lord, and not to men." The paycheck is just an added bonus!

> *Let him provide for the sick, the children, the guests, and the poor, with all care, knowing that, without doubt, he will have to give an account of all these things on judgment day.*

Taking special care of those who need it, like the sick, elderly, and children, is directly ministering to Christ. In Matthew 25.40, He says, "Inasmuch as ye have done it unto one of the least of these my brethren, ye have done it unto me."

> *Let him regard all the tools of the monastery and all its substance, as if they were sacred vessels of the altar. Let him neglect nothing and let him not give way to greed, nor let him be*

wasteful and a squanderer of the goods of the monastery; but let him do all things in due measure and according to the bidding of his Abbot.

When I was younger, my older brother worked with a lot of tools, and he had a very hot temper. When he got angry, tools would fly across the garage. Needless to say, I became rather adept at dodging them. We need to treat tools with respect, especially when they are not our tools!

The same can be said of our gifts and talents, the other "tools" that are entrusted to us. We need to be careful how we use them. Some of us who have spent time in prison have used our gifts and talents illegally, landing us in trouble with the law. When we use our gifts properly and with wisdom, they will flourish. Let's look at the next paragraph.

Above all things, let him be humble; and if he does not have the things to give, let him answer with a kind word, because it is written: "A good word is above the best gift."

The quote is from the deuterocanonical book Sirach (18.17), which reads, "Lo, is not a word better than a gift? but both are with a justified man." Deuterocanonical books are books that are in the Catholic Bibles, but were removed from the Protestant versions. In former years, the book was titled "Ecclesiasticus" but don't confuse it with "Ecclesiastes," which is a different book. Benedict is saying that kind words go far, and if someone has nothing else to give, at least a kind word will be worth something. Let's look at the next two paragraphs together.

Let him have under his charge everything that the Abbot has entrusted to him, and not presume to meddle with matters forbidden him. Let him give the brethren their apportioned allowance without a ruffle or delay, that they may not be

> *scandalized, mindful of what the Divine Word declares that he who shall scandalize one of these little ones deserves: "It were better for him that a millstone should hang about his neck and that he were drowned in the depth of the sea."*

Here again, Benedict is simply saying that the cellarer needs to do his job as appointed and with all humility. And now, the last paragraph.

> *If the community is large, let assistants be given him, that, with their help, he too may fulfil the office entrusted to him with an even temper. Let the things that are to be given be distributed, and the things that are to be gotten asked for at the proper times, so that nobody may be disturbed or grieved in the house of God.*

Some monasteries are larger, and require more than one person in a job. This may relieve any stress brought on by not being able to fulfill a job. We, too, should not be afraid to ask for help in our daily lives when we need it. Some may see asking for help as a sign of weakness, but I see it as a sign of strength; it takes great strength and self-assurance to be able to ask for help when it is needed.

The last sentence talks about giving and asking for things at the proper times. In a monastery, as in most prisons, the daily schedule is rather regimented. Aside from that kind of "proper time," there are other considerations. For example, if a prison guard is talking to his superior, it would not be a good time to ask him for a favor, lest he appear to be too "soft" on the prisoners. Nor would that be a good time to complain about something that the guard should have taken care of. Taking care to ask for things at the proper times can go a long way in getting what you need.

32

On the Tools and Goods of the Monastery

Monks work, and since they own nothing, the tools with which they work are owned by the monastery.

> *Let the Abbot appoint brothers on whose life and character he can rely, over the property of the monastery in tools, clothing, and things generally, and let him assign to them, as he shall deem proper, all the articles which must be collected after use and stored away. Let the Abbot keep a list of these articles, so that, when the brothers in turn succeed each other in these trusts, he may know what he gave and what he received back. If anyone, however, handles the goods of the monastery slovenly or carelessly let him be reprimanded and if he does not amend let him come under the discipline of the Rule.*

Again, the tools that a monk uses are borrowed from the monastery, and so they need to be treated with care. Isn't everything we have on loan? After all, we came into the world with nothing but our soul, and we shall leave with nothing but our soul. Indeed, our very lives are on loan from God!

In prison, our worldly possessions are often seen as being of greater worth because of the difficulty in obtaining them. One of my prized possessions in prison was a small plastic tube in which I kept my cotton swabs. These tubes had been given to diabetic inmates to keep glucose tablets in them. Shortly after distributing them to the diabetics, the prison realized that the inmates were hiding things in the tubes and using them to transport illegal contraband from the work area to the living area. They were no longer distributed to the inmates, so my tube became a rarity. It's strange that now, outside of prison, I can walk across the street and buy one of these tubes with the glucose tablets and bring it home. I still have my tube from prison!

When we have so little, and when we can acquire so little, even our smallest possessions become much more valuable, and we tend to take better care of them. In prison, people routinely sew and repair shirts and pants that would simply be discarded outside of prison. It is this kind of care, against treating things as disposable that Benedict speaks of here. Taking care of things, especially when they are not ours, helps them last longer. And this becomes very important whether you are a monk living with a vow of poverty, or you are a prisoner, making only thirteen cents an hour.

33

Whether Monks Ought to Have Anything of Their Own

Monks take a vow of poverty, and the reason for this is to increase trust in God to provide. However, occasionally a monk will violate this vow.

> *The vice of personal ownership must by all means be cut out in the monastery by the very root, so that no one may presume to give or receive anything without the command of the Abbot; nor to have anything whatever as his own, neither a book, nor a writing tablet, nor a pen, nor anything else whatsoever, since monks are allowed to have neither their bodies nor their wills in their own power. Everything that is necessary, however, they must look for from the Father of the monastery; and let it not be allowed for anyone to have anything which the Abbot did not give or permit him to have. Let all things be common to all, as it is written. And let no one call or take to himself anything as his own.*
>
> *But if anyone should be found to indulge this most deadly vice, and, having been admonished once and again, does not amend, let him be subjected to punishment.*

Perhaps the most difficult part of this chapter is the statement that the monks "are allowed to have neither their bodies nor their wills in their own power." Does he mean that the monks become mindless followers, without thinking for themselves? No. Benedict is speaking about letting our minds and wills run their own course, without any direction.

We can gain much by simplifying our lives and minimizing

the "things" we collect as we get older. We can also gain much by minimizing the excesses in our mind. This is what meditation helps us do. As we practice meditation, we become more adept at letting distractions go and being focused, more mindful. This is a form of poverty, an austerity of the mind, and we will find that we become much more peaceful and effective as we continue to practice meditation.

Additionally, this lack of ownership is not simply about depriving monks of possessions. Rather, because everything is owned by the community of monks, it helps to develop a sense of interdependence. We learn to rely not only on the help of our brothers, but on Christ as well. Unfortunately, western society tends to teach us the opposite, but learning communal interdependence can really help you grow closer to those around you.

34

Whether All Should Receive in Equal Measure What is Necessary

Some monks may have different needs, and that issue is addressed in this chapter.

> *It is written, "Distribution was made to everyone according as he had need." We do not say by this that respect should be had for persons (God forbid), but regard for infirmities. Let him who has need of less thank God and not give way to sadness, but let him who has need of more, humble himself for his infirmity, and not be elated for the indulgence shown him; and thus all the members will be at peace.*
>
> *Above all, let not the evil of murmuring appear in the least word or sign for any reason whatever. If anyone be found guilty of this, let him be placed under very severe discipline.*

Some monks are much older than others, or may have some disability that prevents them from carrying out the same work or the same amount of work as that assigned to others. When we are young and strong, we should be thankful for our health and vigor. Further, we should not be saying things about others who are unable to do as much as we can. It is a privilege to do work for others, as we are serving Christ in the disabled and infirm.

Likewise, Benedict warns against those with disabilities using their disability to gain favor or to feel more privileged. Rather, he says they should feel humbled.

I have a sleep disorder that causes me to stop breathing when I sleep. Because of this, I have to use a special respirator when I sleep. Having the respirator actually helped me in several situations in prison: it prevented me being housed in a bad area, and it delayed unwanted transfers to other facilities. However, I never felt "lucky" or privileged to have the disorder. On the contrary, it has been a great hindrance. For example, I love camping out in the woods, but if it means I have to tote a generator along just so I can breathe properly when I sleep, I would ruin the rustic experience of camping. I feel humbled by my condition, because it has limited my life in some ways. However, I also feel blessed that it has rarely required special accommodation.

35

On the Weekly Servers in the Kitchen

Just like prisons, most monasteries have a central kitchen where all the food for the monks is prepared, and just like prisons, the "residents" prepare the food.

Let the brothers serve each other so that no one be excused from the work in the kitchen, except on account of sickness or more necessary work, because greater merit and more charity is thereby acquired. Let help be given to the weak, however, that they may not do this work with sadness; but let all have help according to the size of the community and the circumstances of the place. If the community is large, let the Cellarer be excused from the kitchen, or if, as we have said, any are engaged in more urgent work; let the rest serve each other in charity.

Let him who is finishing the weekly service, do the cleaning on Saturday. Let him wash the towels with which the brothers wipe their hands and feet. Let him who is leaving, as well as him who is to come in, wash the feet of all. Let him return the utensils of his department to the Cellarer clean and whole. Let the Cellarer give the same tools to the one who is coming in, so that he may know what he gives and what he receives back.

An hour before meal time let the weekly servers receive each a cup of drink and a piece of bread over the prescribed portion, that they may serve their brethren at mealtime without murmuring and undue strain. On solemn feast days, however, let them abstain until after Mass.

As soon as the morning office on Sunday is ended, let the weekly servers who come in and who go out, cast themselves upon their knees in the oratory before all, asking for their prayers. Let him who is ending the weekly service, say the following verse: You are blessed, Lord God, who have helped me and comforted me. *The one going out having said this three times and received the blessing, let the one who is coming in follow and say:* God, come to my assistance; O Lord, make haste to help me. *And let this also be repeated three times by all, and having received the blessing let him enter upon his weekly service.*

When I was in prison, working in the kitchen was a much sought-after job. The reason for this was the access to food. There were always leftovers, and even though it was against regulations, the workers would always come to their cells with bags of food left over from the morning or evening meal. They could use the food themselves, cooking it into soups or burritos, or they could even sell the food to others by trading it for other things. If you are in prison, I am sure you see this happening where you are at as well.

Just like the others, I had my time in the kitchen as well. I was used to being a clerk by that time, typing forms for vocational instructors and teachers. When I was assigned to the kitchen, I was assigned as a clerk, typing the various forms used in the kitchen. The clerk's daily work is done within about a half hour. However, I was assigned to the kitchen all day, so I had to "hang out." Well, I don't like to be too idle for very long, so I asked my supervisor if I could work where the trays were washed (considered to be one of the worst assignments in the kitchen). He looked at me as if I had Spock-ears and two antennae growing out of my head! He said if I wanted to, he had nothing against it. So I did.

I was really glad I had requested to work there, because I had lots of interaction with the other inmates when they handed in their trays. They were quite surprised when I first started working there because when they handed me their tray, I would always reply, "Thank you." I don't think they were used to that. Even the other workers commented that I was going to be saying about a thousand thank yous each night. I did, and eventually (although slowly), I started to get replies. At first, they were just nods of the head, but then some would reply, "You're welcome." In a small way, my work in the kitchen had caused a small transformation on the yard, and I was very happy for it.

Even if we work at the worst job with little or no pay (I made 18 cents an hour in the prison kitchen!), we can make a difference in some small way, and it is through the serving of others that we will find the greatest change, perhaps not in who we are serving, but in ourselves.

It is also interesting to note that the prayers said by the servers who are starting their week in the kitchen is the same as the beginning of the Daily Office prayers. Though it is sometimes difficult, our work, whether exciting or mundane, can be a prayer when offered to God.

36

On the Sick Brethren

Illness is inevitable with all of us, and it is no different with monks.

> *Before and above all things, care must be taken of the sick, that they be served in the same way as Christ is served; because He said, "I was sick and you visited Me." And "As long as you did it to one of the least of my brothers, you did it to Me." But let the sick themselves also consider that they are served for the honor of God, and let them not grieve their brothers who serve them by unnecessary demands. These must, however, be patiently borne with, because from such as these a more bountiful reward is gained. Let the Abbot's greatest concern, therefore, be that they suffer no neglect.*
>
> *Let a cell be set apart for the sick brethren, and a God-fearing, diligent, and careful attendant be appointed to serve them. Let the use of the bath be offered to the sick as often as it is useful, but let it be granted more rarely to the healthy and especially the young. Thus also let the use of meat be granted to the sick and to the very weak for their recovery. But when they have been restored let them all abstain from meat in the usual manner.*
>
> *But let the Abbot exercise the utmost care that the sick are not neglected by the Cellarer or the attendants, because whatever his disciples do wrongly falls back on him.*

Much of this chapter is either common sense or repeats general concepts covered before. Chapter 34 covered the disabled, and many of the same concepts apply here. There is one interesting note, and it is dietary. It is this phrase: "...let them all abstain from meat in the usual manner." The monks were vegetarians.

The reason for this may be due to general availability of meat (or at least healthy meat) at the time of the writing of the Rule. Meat was considered a luxury, as it still is in many parts of the world. Thus, to always to be dining on meat would give the impression that the monks were not actually abstaining from luxuries as much as one might think. In a more modern society that employs factory-farming methods, meat is not really a luxury. I would not necessarily read into this that we should all be vegetarians. Paul wrote in his letter to the Romans (Romans 14.15): "For if, because of thy meat, thy brother be grieved, thou walkest not now according to charity. Destroy not him with thy meat, for whom Christ died. Let not then our good be evil spoken of. For the kingdom of God is not meat and drink; but justice, and peace, and joy in the Holy Ghost." In other words, if it's causing a problem with someone, don't do it. The meat itself is not evil, but the intent with which one eats (see verse 20 of the same chapter: "Destroy not the work of God for meat. All things indeed are clean: but it is evil for that man who eateth with offence."). Benedict required that the monks ordinarily not eat meat, and it may very well be due to the "luxury" status of meat at that time, or simply because the earlier Desert Fathers ate mostly bread and water with a few vegetables every now and then. There's nothing wrong with a little luxury now and then, as long as it does not come at the expense of one's faith. Even Christ allowed the expensive perfume to be placed on his feet (Luke 7.38).

37

On the Aged and Children

We've discussed taking care of the ill, and now Benedict discusses taking care of the elderly and the children. As I mentioned in an earlier chapter, it was common in the days of Benedict to have children being raised by monks in a monastery.

> *Although human nature is of itself drawn to feel compassion for these life-periods, namely, old age and childhood, still, let the decree of the Rule make provision also for them. Let their natural weakness be always taken into account and let the strictness of the Rule not be kept with them in respect to food, but let there be a tender regard in their behalf and let them eat before regular hours.*

The elderly and the young require a special amount of attention and care, not only in physical means, but socially, mentally, etc. As I write this, my mother has just recently celebrated her seventy-seventh birthday. She is in excellent health for her age, but there are still certain things that are noticeably different. She has to walk a little more slowly than she did when she used to chase us kids about the house. But there are other differences. I have noticed that she is more sensitive to the problems of the world in general, and to the sometimes strained relationships within our family. Things that years ago would not have noticeably bothered her seem to bother her more visibly today.

We know that children do not typically have the same intellectual capacity as we do, and because of that, certain things have to be explained in more detail, or sometimes in more general ways. With the elderly, we may have to be more careful discussing things that might upset them.

My incarceration was quite a shock to most of my family, but most of all to my father. I knew he would not take it well, so I communicated with the rest of the family first, and we all decided that the family would all be there to help him cope with the news. I know it upset him greatly, and I still feel bad about causing him so much grief. Most of us who have been in or are still in prison know that we never thought about how our actions would affect others. Now, we have the capacity to change that. Keep in your thoughts the people in your life, and how your actions or conversations will affect them. It will make for a much smoother ride through life.

38

On the Weekly Reader

In case you're wondering, the term "Weekly Reader" does not refer to a magazine. Benedict describes the role of the Weekly Reader in a monastery.

> *Reading must not be lacking at the table of the brothers when they are eating. Neither let anyone who may decide to take up the book venture to read there; but let him who is to read for the whole week enter upon that office on Sunday. After Mass and Communion let him ask all to pray for him that God may ward off from him the spirit of pride. And let the following verse be said three times by all in the oratory, he beginning it:* Lord, open my lips, and my mouth shall proclaim Your praise, *and thus having received the blessing let him enter upon the reading.*
>
> *Let the deepest silence be maintained that no whispering or voice be heard except that of the reader alone. But let the brethren so help each other to what is needed for eating and drinking, that no one need ask for anything. If, however, anything should be needed, let it be asked for by means of a sign of any kind rather than a sound. And let no one presume to ask any questions there, either about the book or anything else, in order that no cause to speak be given, unless the Superior wishes to say a few words for edification.*
>
> *Let the brother who is reader for the week take a little bread and wine before he begins to read, on account of Holy Communion, and lest it should be too hard for him to fast so long. Afterward, however, let him take his meal in the kitchen with the weekly servers and the waiters.*

The brothers, however, will not read or sing in order, but only those who edify their hearers.

The weekly readers read while the rest of the monks are eating. Note the verse that they are required to intone is the same verse that all the monks intone at the first prayers of the day: "O Lord, open my lips..." This is said because the monks have been in silence all throughout the night.

The silence required at the table had, in later years, prompted some monks to either develop or adapt a type of communication using their hands, similar to sign language for the hearing impaired.

The dining rooms, or "chow halls" of most prisons are anything but quiet. Of course, no one is reading to the inmates, so there is really no need. The only real respite is granted during "lock-downs" when all the inmates on the yard are confined to their cells for security reasons (i.e. after a riot or other violent incident). During these times, the food trays are delivered to the cells through a small opening in the door. My cell mate and I would eat in almost complete silence, and it was quite peaceful.

Silence is important in our lives. In a way, it causes us to take notice of ourselves, and perhaps that is the reason so many people shun silence: perhaps they fear confronting themselves, what is inside. It is only by way of this confrontation with ourselves, however, that we can really learn to resolve our deepest issues. Additionally, it is through silence that we are more open to communication from others. It's very hard to listen to someone else when we are talking. Perhaps we have made pleas, requests, and cries to God, but it seems as though He never answers us. Perhaps we are not listening because we are too busy "talking" in our own lives. Remember where Elijah found God? In I Kings 19.11-12, we read that Elijah was waiting on God. "And he said, Go forth, and stand upon the mount before the Lord. And, behold, the Lord passed by, and a great and strong wind rent the mountains, and brake in pieces the rocks before the Lord; but the Lord was not in the wind: and after the wind an earthquake; but the Lord was not in the earthquake: And after the earthquake a fire; but the Lord was not in the fire: and after the fire a still small voice" (KJV). It was in the "still small voice." We won't find God in the winds, earthquakes, or fires of our lives. We find him in the quiet places.

39

On the Quantity of Food

You may recall the image of Friar Tuck from the various accounts of Robin Hood. In all the accounts I have seen, Friar Tuck was a rather portly fellow, probably given to gluttony now and then. Benedict does his best in this chapter to prevent such a problem.

> *Making allowance for the infirmities of different persons, we believe that for the daily meal, both at the sixth and the ninth hour, two kinds of cooked food are sufficient at all meals; so that he who cannot eat of one, may make his meal of the other. Let two kinds of cooked food, therefore, be sufficient for all the brothers. And if there are fruits or fresh vegetables, a third may be added.*
>
> *Let a pound of bread be sufficient for the day, whether there is only one meal or both dinner and supper. If they are to eat supper, let a third part of the pound be reserved by the Cellarer and be given at supper.*
>
> *If, however, the work has been especially hard, it is left to the discretion and power of the Abbot to add something, if he thinks it is appropriate, barring above all things every excess, that a monk be not overtaken by indigestion. For nothing is so contrary to Christians as excess, as our Lord says: "See that your hearts be not overcharged with over-eating."*
>
> *Let the same quantity of food, however, not be served out to young children but less than what is served to older ones, observing measure in all things.*
>
> *But let all except the very weak and the sick abstain altogether from eating the flesh of four-footed animals.*

The addition of the second cooked dish is on account of those who may have specific food allergies or who may not be able to handle the spice of one of the dishes. Many a night I went a little hungrier in prison because salsa was placed on the dinner tray mixed with the main course, and I happen to be allergic to cilantro, which was one of the ingredients in the salsa used at the prison. Those who have not been to prison may wonder, "Can't you just ask for a tray with no salsa?" The reply would certainly be along the lines of, "Do you think you're special?" Well, I did, in fact, think I was special, but I wasn't about to say that!

A pound of bread may seem like quite a lot (a typical loaf of bread is about a pound), but the kind of bread baked in a monastery was likely a bit more dense than the standard sandwich bread available at your local grocer. Thus, the pound of bread for the day would look smaller.

Benedict takes special care to prevent gluttony, or "over-eating," among his brethren. There is a certain balance we can achieve in our lives by avoiding over-indulgence in any particular area, including food. For example, I love sitting at my computer and writing. However, if I spent all day at the computer, I would be much fatter than I already am, and I would not have much of a social life. I have to keep in contact with family and friends, and I try to get outside and exercise at least once a day. I try to keep a balance, avoiding over-indulgence.

Meditation will help us keep a balance in our lives as well. If we are like most people, we are constantly surrounded by various stressors, things that increase our stress level (perhaps fights, noise, the guards, a cell mate who won't keep the cell clean, or for those outside prison, our finances, bills, problems at work and home). By taking some time out twice a day to quiet our bodies and our minds, we will find that we are able to cope better in stressful situations the rest of the time. If we have no outlet for that stress, it will build up inside and cause all kinds of problems. Meditation is not "covering up" the stress, but rather letting the body take a rest so that it can cope with the stress during the rest of the day. You may even find that, after some period of regular meditation practice, your blood pressure goes down and your health improves. Take some time out, twenty minutes twice a day, to meditate and tackle the "over-indulgences" that life likes to throw our way.

40

On the Quantity of Drink

Speaking of Friar Tuck… Well, suffice it to say that things like wine need to be controlled.

> *"Every one has his proper gift from God, one after this manner and another after that." It is with some hesitation, therefore, that we determine the measure of nourishment for others. However, making allowance for the weakness of the infirm, we think one hemina of wine a day is sufficient for each one. But to whom God grants the endurance of abstinence, let them know that they will have their special reward. If the circumstances of the place, or the work, or the summer's heat should require more, let that depend on the judgment of the Superior, who must above all things see to it, that excess or drunkenness do not creep in.*
>
> *Although we read that wine is not at all proper for monks, yet, because monks in our times cannot be persuaded of this, let us agree to this, at least, that we do not drink to fullness, but sparingly; because "wine makes even wise men fall off." But where the poverty of the place will not permit this measure to be had, but much less, or none at all, let those who live there bless God and murmur not. This we charge above all things, that they live without murmuring.*

Here we see a different side of Benedict. Even though he would rather say that monks should not drink wine, he realizes that the monks of his day cannot seem to do without it, and so he "gives in" by granting them some to enjoy, much as wine was enjoyed in Christ's day, but not enough to cause any problems with those who may have a problem with alcohol.

You may be wondering, how much is a "hemina?" Good question. No one knows, but it is thought by some to be roughly ten fluid ounces. Certainly not enough to get drunk on. However, it must be something of a little pleasure to have a small amount each day.

The little pleasures in life are necessary sometimes to help us maintain our sanity. After spending ten years in prison, some may have found it odd that I would take so much pleasure in a pint of ice cream. Oh, the bliss! After waiting ten years, that was the most wonderful ice cream I think I will ever have in my life! The little pleasures in life are made more pleasurable by our waiting in between. I am reminded of Easter as a child, when we were allowed to indulge in whatever we had given up for Lent (chocolate, gum, or some other little pleasure). It was so much sweeter after a long wait!

In Antoine de Saint-Exupéry's book, "The Little Prince," he describes something like this, and this particular passage always reminded me of something Christ might have said to his apostles before he left. In the story, the narrator has crashed his airplane in the desert, and after a week or so of attempting to repair it, his water supply has run out. The Little Prince has been with him the whole time, and it seems he knew there was a water supply just a little walk away, but he does not tell the narrator this until his water supply runs out. He finally leads the narrator to the well. Together, they delight in the sound of the rusty pulley on the well. "I am thirsty for this water," said the Little Prince. "Give me some of it to drink."

As they pull water up from the well, the rusty pulley makes a sound, and the Little Prince comments later on it: "It is just as it is with the water. Because of the pulley, and the rope, what you gave me to drink was like music." When the Little Prince says he is returning to his planet, his companion says that he will look to the stars to remember him, and the Little Prince says, " … I, too, shall look at the stars. All the stars will be wells of water with a rusty pulley. All the stars will pour out fresh water for me to drink…."

Life in prison is all about "doing without." Still, there are occasional little treats, little pleasures that may bring pleasant memories or thoughts to mind. That is something like Benedict's hemina of wine each day. Don't live your life without these pleasures. Even if you're a monk.

41

At What Times Brothers Should Take Their Meals

Life in a monastery is rather regimented, and even the most minute details are scheduled, such as when to eat.

> *From holy Easter until Pentecost let the brothers dine at the sixth hour and take supper in the evening. From Pentecost on, however, during the whole summer, if the monks have no work in the fields and the excess of the heat does not interfere, let them fast on Wednesday and Friday until the ninth hour; but on the other days let them dine at the sixth hour. This sixth hour for dinner is to be continued, if they have work in the fields or the heat of the summer is great. Let the Abbot provide for this; and so let him manage and adapt everything that souls may be saved, and that what the brothers do, they may do without having a reasonable cause to murmur. From the ides of September until the beginning of Lent let them always dine at the ninth hour. During Lent, however, until Easter, let them dine in the evening. But let this evening hour be so arranged that they will not need lamp-light during their meal; but let everything be finished while it is still day. But at all times let the hour of meals, whether for dinner or for supper, be so arranged that everything is done by daylight.*

First, note that the term "ides" basically means the middle of the month, so the "ides of September" would be September 15th. Note also that the hours are counted from daylight, so the "sixth hour" is not six o'clock, but rather sometime close to noon, the sixth hour of daylight.

In the monastery, though the time to eat changes with the

seasons, the weather, and the type of work done by the monks, for each of those circumstances, the time is set.

Nourishment comes in many different forms, and food is just one of them. We also have intellectual nourishment as well as spiritual nourishment. However, we may often neglect these other types of nourishment. When we have a habit of forgetting or neglecting necessary nourishment, we need to make a schedule of sorts, to make sure we always do these things at the same time every day. In this way, we form a habit, and we will not neglect the things we need.

When I meditate, I try to do it at the same time every day. In prison, this was much easier, as the schedule in prison is so regimented. As I mentioned earlier, "count times" worked out best for me, as did the early mornings before everyone got up and started making noise.

42

That No One Speak After Compline

Compline is the term typically used for the last office of the evening, before going to bed. There is another office, called the night office, that is said before morning, but Compline is usually said as one is first going to bed for the evening. Its name comes from the same word as "complete."

> *Monks should always be given to silence, especially, however, during the hours of the night. Therefore, on every day, whether of fast or of a mid-day meal, as soon as they have risen from their evening meal, let all sit together in one place, and let one read the Conferences or the Lives of the Fathers, or something else that will edify the hearers; not, however, the Heptateuch or the Books of the Kings, because it would not be wholesome for weak minds to hear this part of the Scripture at that hour; they should, however, be read at other times. But if it was a fast-day, then, when Vespers have been said, and after a short interval, let them next come together for the reading of the Conferences, as we have said; and when the four or five pages have been read, or as much as the hour will permit, and all have assembled in one place during the time of the reading, let him also come who was perchance engaged in work enjoined on him. All, therefore, having assembled in one place, let them say Compline, and after going out from Compline, let there be no more permission from that time on for anyone to say anything.*
>
> *If, however, anyone is found to break this rule, let him undergo heavy punishment, unless the needs of guests should arise, or the Abbot should perhaps give a command to anyone. But let even this be done with the utmost gravity and moderation.*

This chapter includes mention of several books which may be foreign to most people today. The book referred to as "Conferences" is a book by John Cassian containing teachings of the Egyptian desert fathers. "Lives of the Fathers" would be, somewhat obviously, a similar book containing biographical descriptions of some of the early church "fathers." The "Heptateuch" is just a Greek name for the first seven books of the Old Testament, and the "Books of the Kings" would be I Kings and II Kings from the Old Testament. A cursory glance at the stories in these books, and one can see why Benedict recommends against reading them just before bedtime.

Note that a very great solemnity falls upon the monastery when it is in darkness. Even in the previous chapter, there is mention by Benedict that "the hour, whether for supper or for dinner, be so arranged that everything will be done by daylight." Indeed, physical darkness has its spiritual parallel, and it is during the darknesses of our lives that we need to reflect on the brighter times. When darkness happens in our lives, we become austere, and perhaps more silent. It is a time when we might listen a little more for the Voice of God in our lives, and to do that we need to maintain a level of silence.

When we are incarcerated, we are in a very dark place in our lives. We may laugh and appear to have fun with our friends on the yard, but the truth is that most of us would rather be outside the prison walls than inside. We can take the time inside prison to not only reflect on how our actions led us to be incarcerated, but also to listen deeply for the Voice of God in all things.

As with all darknesses, we should also remember that daylight is coming. It may take a while, but it will come.

43

On Those Who Are Tardy in Coming to the Work of God or to Table

As with all structured environments, lateness in the monastery is not smiled upon. The same holds true for prison. This is a somewhat lengthy chapter, so I will tackle it in two separate pieces.

> *As soon as the signal for the time of the divine office is heard, let everyone, leaving whatever he has in his hands, hurry with all speed, yet with gravity, that there may be no cause for levity. Therefore, let nothing be preferred to the Work of God. If at Matins anyone comes after the Gloria of the 94th psalm, which on that account we wish to be much drawn out and said slowly, let him not stand in his place in the choir; but let him stand last of all, or in a place which the Abbot has set apart for such careless ones, that he may be seen by him and by all, until, the Work of God being ended, he makes satisfaction by public penance. The reason, however, why we think they should stand in the last place, or apart from the rest, is this, that seen by all they may amend for very shame. For if they stayed outside the oratory, there might be one who would go back to sleep, or anyhow would seat himself outside, indulge in vain gossip, and give a "chance to the devil." Let him go inside, therefore, that he may not lose the whole, and may amend for the future.*
>
> *At the day hours, however, whoever doth not arrive for the Work of God after the verse and the Gloria of the first psalm, which is said after the verse, let him stand in the last place, according to the rule which we stated above; and let him not*

> *attempt to join the choir of the chanters until he has made satisfaction, unless the Abbot's permission has given him leave to do so, with the understanding that he atone the fault afterwards.*

Upon reading this chapter, you may think that monastic life is rather like the military life. Indeed, it is, but the monks fight the spiritual battle. We also fight a spiritual battle every day, and when immediate, tangible confirmation of our efforts is not readily obvious, we may become disheartened or even lazy in our efforts. However, in our daily lives, there is no one to "police" our spiritual efforts; that task is left to us. In the monastery, there is discipline, but without the monastery, we are left to discipline ourselves.

One can take from this chapter the concept that satisfaction must be made for our faults. This is something we may often think about while incarcerated. Our faults may be many, or serious, or even both, and we may never feel that there is anything we can do in this lifetime to "make satisfaction" for the harm we have caused. In the spiritual sense, the debt is paid if we accept it as a gift from Christ. However, some satisfaction should still be paid (note that King David had to make satisfaction for his sin, despite being forgiven by God: see II Samuel 12.13-14).

It may be particularly difficult for us to make direct satisfaction for our past actions, but indirect satisfaction can be made. One can do other good in the world, above what is required, to benefit others.

On a personal note, there are people living in this world who are victims of my crime. I cannot make satisfaction to them. First, there is nothing I can do to take away the damage I have caused. Second, it would be highly inappropriate for me to contact them. The best I can do is "make satisfaction" by what has recently been termed "paying it forward." In other words, do something to help someone today, maybe even a smile or a kind word. In this way, we might begin to put more kindness into the world than we may have taken out in the past. Then, perhaps some day soon, the balance sheet will be in the black.

Let's look at the second half of this chapter.

> *If anyone does not come to table before the verse, so that all may say the verse and pray together and sit down to table at the same time, let him be twice corrected for this, if he failed to come through his own fault and negligence. If he does not amend after this, let him not be permitted to eat at the common table; but separated from the company of all, let him eat alone, his portion of wine being taken from him, until he has made satisfaction and has amended. In like manner let him suffer who is not present also at the verse which is said after the meal.*
>
> *And let no one presume to take food or drink before or after the appointed time. But if anything should be offered to a brother by the Superior and he refuses to accept it, and afterwards desires what at first he refused or anything else, let him receive nothing at all, until he makes due satisfaction.*

Benedict mentions here the importance of coming to the table before the first verse. It is important to understand that the verse is a community prayer, and failing to join the community in the verse is, in a sense, failing the community. And since it is also a prayer to God, it is also, in a sense, failing God. For these reasons, Benedict places great importance on being punctual for community prayer.

We can see here the importance of community. In view of the remainder of the chapter, we can also see how our actions can affect so many other people. Think about crime for a moment. When someone decides to rob a store, even though he may not have caused any physical harm to the cashier in the store, the robber may have so frightened the cashier that he can no longer work at that store, or any store, and may not be able to find work without having an overwhelming fear. Additionally, when the robber is caught, it is not just he who is punished, but his family and friends now have to deal with his incarceration. We may think that our actions are only affecting us, but they affect many more. The same is true of our bad actions that may be lawful as well. Our indiscretions, or other morally wrong behaviors may adversely affect far more people than we can imagine. Ethics teaches us that the whole community can be affected by the unethical practices of one person. And that is why satisfaction is needed.

Today, think about some past actions, perhaps morally wrong behaviors, unethical actions, or even illegal things you may have done. Now, think of how you can make some satisfaction for them, either directly or indirectly. A large debt is not paid off in one day, so begin today to make a positive difference in those around you, and before you know it you'll be back in the black.

44

How the Excommunicated Make Satisfaction

The term "excommunication" takes on a significantly different meaning in The Rule than that of modern definitions. Herein, it refers to those undergoing a separation from the other brethren in the monastery. In a sense, those serving sentences in prison are "excommunicated" from society. Previously, we have read that those undergoing punishment are to make satisfaction. You may have been asking yourself exactly how they are to make this satisfaction, and the answer follows.

> *Whoever is excommunicated for graver faults from the oratory and the table, let him, at the time that the Work of God is celebrated in the oratory, lie stretched, face down in silence before the door of the oratory at the feet of all who come out. And let him do this until the Abbot judges that it is enough. When he then comes at the Abbot's bidding, let him cast himself at the Abbot's feet, then at the feet of all, that they may pray for him. If then the Abbot orders it, let him be received back into the choir in the place which the Abbot shall direct; yet so that he does not presume to intone a psalm or a lesson or anything else in the oratory, unless the Abbot again bids him to do so. Then, at all the Hours, when the Work of God is ended, let him cast himself on the ground in the place where he stands, and thus let him make satisfaction, until the Abbot again bids him finally to cease from this penance.*
>
> *But let those who are excommunicated for lighter faults from the table only make satisfaction in the oratory, as long as the Abbot commands, and let them perform this until he gives his blessing and says, "It is enough."*

The final statement, a potential quote from the Abbot, always reminds me of Mark 14.41. Here, Christ is in the garden praying, and the apostles are sleeping. He has caught them now twice already, and on the third time...: "And he cometh the third time, and saith to them: Sleep ye now, and take your rest. It is enough: the hour is come: behold the Son of man shall be betrayed into the hands of sinners." It is enough. I think Christ is saying that they have done all they can do, and that is what the Abbot is saying as well.

To "lie stretched," or prostrate before someone's feet is a clear sign of humility. In essence, you are acknowledging your humanity and frailty. The very word "*humility*" comes from the same word "humus" meaning "dirt or earth." *Humility* is recognizing that we are *human* and made of *humus* (dirt). In Genesis 2.7, the Bible speaks of God forming man from the ground, from the dirt, and acknowledging that in itself can be rather humiliating! In the same way, we are humiliated to some degree (or should be) when we are guilty of doing wrong. There is a 12-step group that uses the phrase "From shame to grace" as one of their slogans. That is exactly what is reflected here between the monk and the Abbot. At first, the monk feels shame for his improper actions, and he acknowledges his humanity by way of his humility. Then, the Abbot provides the "grace" for the monk to resume his former standing.

And, of course, this is a reflection of what happens when we transgress the commandments of God. We feel shame, we recognize our humanity via humility, and we are given grace to restore us to our previous standing. And what better way to recognize our humanity than to get close to the humus!

Outside of the monastery, we can acknowledge our humanity by kneeling and praying. And perhaps we can say, as Abraham did to God (Genesis 18.27): "...I am dust and ashes."

45

On Those Who Commit A Fault in the Oratory

The Oratory is the place where the prayers are said (Oration comes from a Latin word meaning to pray). Thus, a mistake in the Oratory refers to mistakes made while praying. This chapter, one of the shortest in the Rule, contains what is probably the most controversial of all the statements in the Rule.

> *If anyone while he recites a psalm, a responsory, an antiphon, or a lesson, makes a mistake, and does not humble himself there before all by making satisfaction, let him undergo a greater punishment, because he would not correct by humility what he did wrong through negligence. But let boys be whipped for such a fault.*

I am always somewhat taken aback by the final statement. It seems a rather serious punishment for a simple accident!

First of all, I'd like to calm your concerns by letting you know that, to my knowledge, the whippings of boys are not carried out in today's monasteries. But one must ask, why was it carried out in the first place? What kind of person would allow such a thing?

In order to understand this, we need to understand the importance of the "Work of God" prayers, or the Liturgy of the Hours. This is a liturgy, a "service" being given to God, and it was considered vitally important that great care be taken when speaking to God under any circumstances. Since most people, monks included, have difficulty grasping the relevance of penalties to be exacted in the afterlife, the penalty was made more immediate. Thus, the threat of punishment was a way of ensuring that the monks would take greater care intoning their prayers.

Additionally, the whipping of boys was considered normal discipline until just the last century.

Thankfully, we don't have to deal with whippings over mistakes made while intoning the Divine Office. So you may be asking yourself, "What possible relevance does this have to me? Since God is a loving God, how can I possibly conceive of a God Who punishes people for making mistakes when praying to Him?"

In my own practice, I place great importance on praying to God, but in a different sense. I find that it is very important for me to feel what I am saying, and I need to pay great attention to my words to make sure they are not "vain repetitions." Jesus warns us not to pray using "vain repetitions" (Matthew 6.7 KJV). Note that he does not say to avoid repetition, but "vain" repetitions, or repetitions that become rote. Praying for something repeatedly is actually encouraged (see Luke 18.1-8). However, we need to make sure that our words are reflecting what we are saying. Otherwise, they become "vain repetitions." After all, which would be worse, a whipping, or a God who does not listen?

46

On Those Who Fail in Any Other Matters

The previous few chapters have covered punishments for specific failures, and this chapter covers punishment for all the other cases. This is the final chapter in this section on punishments (I thought I'd show you a little light at the end of the tunnel!).

> *If anyone while engaged in any work, in the kitchen, in the cellar, in serving, in the bakery, in the garden, at any art or work in any place whatever, commits a fault, or breaks or loses anything, or transgresses in any way whatever, and he does not immediately come before the Abbot and the community, and of his own accord confess his offense and make satisfaction, and it becomes known through another, let him be subjected to a greater correction.*
>
> *If, however, the cause of the offense is secret, let him disclose it to the Abbot alone, or to his spiritual Superiors, who know how to heal their own wounds, and not expose and make public those of others.*

I recall during my arrest that the police officers told me, "If you just tell us everything, then it will be easier on you." While that may not be the best legal advice, it certainly clears the conscience and it shows that you are truly sorry for what you did. As a matter of fact, I tried to plead guilty when I was first arraigned in court, but my attorney wouldn't let me! He told me that I would automatically get the maximum if I decided to plead guilty, and so I should hold out for a deal! In the end, I'm glad I held out, but I had already acknowledged to God and to myself the nature of my transgressions, and was beginning to receive God's grace in healing.

The second paragraph here discusses coming to the Abbot in the role of confessor. We can transgress in our thoughts, by thinking badly about someone or having thoughts of lust or violence toward another. The Catholic Church has for centuries taught confession via a priest. Aside from the theological reasons, there are other advantages to this, the main advantage being that it really helps you deal with the issue and accept it once it's been verbalized to another. Even the 12-step groups have acknowledged this, as one of the steps is "Admitted to God, to ourselves, and to another human being the exact nature of our wrongs." We may feel uncomfortable about discussing our issues with another person, and that is why quite often a Catholic priest is a good candidate (since they have a vow not to divulge what is discussed in confession). You may even be concerned that the priest will be shocked at what you tell him. Trust me: they've heard it all! I thought the same way, and when I went to my first confession in thirty years, I brought a hand-written list with me! The priest did not appear shocked at all, but seemed to genuinely understand human nature and my need for forgiveness.

Unfortunately, though many prisons have chaplains, many do not have priests or chaplains to help in this situation. If you are incarcerated, it may be best to wait until you can confide in someone you know. Even making an appointment to see a psychologist in prison might not be good enough, as the appointment schedules are rarely confidential, and the information gleaned from a discussion could end up in your file, possibly impacting a release decision by a parole board.

For those who are also meditating, you may find that there are certain "issues" coming up during your meditation, and it may be that you feel you cannot get "past" those issues. That is usually a sign that the issue needs to be dealt with, and that might mean that you need to discuss it with someone.

47

On Giving the Signal for the Time of the Work of God

If you've ever lived near a church or monastery, you have likely heard the bells ringing at various times of the day. In most monasteries, bells are used as the "signal" for the prayer times.

> *Let it be the Abbot's care that the time for the Work of God be announced both by day and by night; either to announce it himself, or to entrust this charge to a careful brother that everything may be done at the proper time.*
>
> *Let those who have been ordered, chant the psalms or the antiphons in their turn after the Abbot. No one, however, should presume to sing or read unless he is able to perform this office that the hearers may be edified; and let it be done with humility, gravity, and reverence by him whom the Abbot has ordered.*

In prison, everything is carefully scheduled. Eat at this time, sleep at this time, get up at this time, go to work at this time, shower at this time, etc. One of the reasons for this is because prisons typically house LOTS of people, and coordinating activities among so many individuals requires a lot of regimentation, especially in scheduling.

Additionally, proper scheduling is important in a monastery in order to bolster the feeling of community, not just within a single monastery, but throughout the world. This is because all the monasteries say prayers at the same time. Thus, when Prime is being said in one monastery, they should know that their brothers in all the other monasteries (at least in their time zone) are joined with them in common prayer. And those who are in a time zone three hours different are likely also praying, though one of the other offices. This community helps unite the monks, not just to each other in the monastery, but to the other monasteries as well.

Benedict also discusses the importance of having someone read (or sing) who can "edify the hearers." We have all heard people who read out loud, and either read too slowly, or possibly with no feeling or emotion in their voice. When these people read, it is very difficult for us to listen to them or to pay attention. For that reason, Benedict underscores the importance of having someone who can read (or sing) in a way that will "edify" those who are listening.

In a deeper sense, we may work with different people, some of whom have personalities that clash with ours, and some with whom we may get along rather well. When we are talking or discussing things with people, we need to make sure that the manner in which we are speaking will "edify" the hearer. In other words, we need to make sure that we are considering the personality of each person, and possibly adjusting our speech or behavior accordingly. For example, I have some friends with whom I can joke around and poke fun at. I made the drastic mistake once of assuming that one of my friends was OK with that. In a fit of rage, he turned around and hit me! We had a long talk afterwards, and when he apologized, I told him that the fault was really mine as well, since I misread him. Ever since then, I've tried to be careful to "read" the other person and their personality, making adjustments as needed. Or, as Paul so aptly said, "I became all things to all men, that I might save all." (I Corinthians 9.22)

48

On the Daily Work

Most people tend to imagine monks sitting around all day, praying and reading the Bible. In fact, many monasteries have the monks engaged in manual labor. Due to the length of this chapter, I will discuss it in three parts.

> *Idleness is the enemy of the soul; and therefore the brothers ought to be employed in manual labor at certain times, at others, in devout reading. Hence, we believe that the time for each will be properly ordered by the following arrangement; namely, that from Easter until the calends of October, they go out in the morning from the first until about the fourth hour, to do the necessary work, but that from the fourth until about the sixth hour they devote to reading. After the sixth hour, however, when they have risen from table, let them rest in their beds in complete silence; or if, perhaps, anyone desires to read for himself, let him so read that he does not disturb others. Let None be said somewhat earlier, about the middle of the eighth hour; and then let them work again at what is necessary until Vespers.*
>
> *If, however, the needs of the place, or poverty should require that they do the work of gathering the harvest themselves, let them not be downcast, for then are they monks in truth, if they live by the work of their hands, as did also our forefathers and the Apostles. However, on account of the faint-hearted let all things be done with moderation.*

First, a reminder that the "Calends" refers to the beginning of the month. It is the Latin word from which we get the word "calendar."

Easter through October would be the warmer months of the year, and so the labor is done in the morning hours, when it is likely to be a little cooler, as well as in the evening hours. An interesting note: Benedict mentions moving "None" a little earlier. By definition, None should be the ninth hour of the day, but it's movement earlier during the warmer months prompted the invention of the term "noon" in English, which now refers to 12:00 P.M., quite a bit earlier than the ninth hour of the day (unless the sun rises at 3:00 AM!).

Benedict places emphasis on the importance of gathering the harvest. The early monks and desert fathers (called "the Fathers" by Benedict) lived alone in the desert, and would have to do all of the gathering and harvesting of food themselves, relying completely on God to provide. Benedict offers some ease of living by way of community, but mentions that the monks should not complain should they have to harvest the food, as this would put them nearer to the conditions of the desert fathers.

I am reminded here of a recent trip I took to the local county aid office. I was unemployed at the time and felt very bad about having to obtain financial aid from the county in order to have enough money to eat. I had mentioned to the social worker that I was willing to work or perform any kind of office jobs if needed. While I was awaiting my final documents, I overheard someone in the lobby complaining that they were going to make him come to the office for five days a month and pick up trash, just so he could get his financial assistance. He wasn't complaining because he was incapable of work; his complaint was that he shouldn't have to work for food because the government should be supplying it to him!

Those of us who are capable of working for our food, let us be thankful for that work, and the food will taste even sweeter coming from our own labors!

From the calends of October until the beginning of Lent, let them apply themselves to reading until the second hour is complete. At the second hour let Tierce be said, and then let all be employed in the work which has been assigned to them until the ninth hour. When, however, the first signal for the hour of None has been given, let each one leave off from work and be ready when the second signal shall strike. But after their meal let them devote themselves to reading or the psalms.

During the Lenten season let them be employed in reading from morning until the third hour, and until the tenth hour let them do the work which is imposed on them. During these days of Lent let all receive books from the library, and let them read them through in order. These books are to be given out at the beginning of the Lenten season.

Above all, let one or two of the seniors be appointed to go about the monastery during the time that the brothers devote to reading and take notice, lest perhaps a slothful brother be found who gives himself up to idleness or vain talk, and does not attend to his reading, and is unprofitable, not only to himself, but disturbs others also. If such a one be found (which God forbid), let him be punished once and again. If he does not amend, let him come under the correction of the Rule in such a way that others may fear. And let not brother join brother at unreasonable hours.

During the colder months, the monks read in the morning (while it's still chilly outside), then work during the warmest parts of the day.

Lent is a time of reflection, especially on the sufferings of Christ. During this time, Benedict recommends each of the monks read a book from the monastery library. As will be covered in the following chapter, each of the monks is supposed to offer something, and I have offered reading in the past. Not reading in general, but specifically reading something of a spiritually edifying nature. For example, I have chosen works by Thomas Merton, and the book "The Cloud of Unknowing" (which I have not yet read – it's waiting for the approaching Lent!). I would recommend this practice as well. If you want to start on something not as deep, try some simpler works. While some prison libraries do not carry religious books, there are many agencies that send books for free to prisoners. Check with your local mail regulations to make sure you can receive these books, and write to one of the organizations, making sure to mention any special limitations or requirements your facility may have (such as only allowing paperback books, or books below a certain weight).

> *On Sunday also let all devote themselves to reading, except those who are appointed to the various functions. But if anyone should be so careless and slothful that he will not or cannot meditate or read, let some work be given him to do, that he may not be idle.*
>
> *Let such work or charge be given to the weak and the sickly brothers, that they are neither idle, nor so wearied with the strain of work that they are driven away. Their weakness must be taken into account by the Abbot.*

Finally, we see here that Benedict regards Sunday as the day of rest, so the brethren are asked to read or engage in some light task. We should always remember to keep part of our schedule to recreation and relaxation. This is how we keep our stress low and our sanity in good order!

49

On the Keeping of Lent

Lent is a very important time for Catholics in general, and monks specifically. Lent is the time that we remember Christ's sufferings in the desert for forty days, as well as his sufferings during the passion, leading up to and including his execution by crucifixion.

> *The life of a monk ought always to be a Lenten observance. However, since such virtue is that of few, we advise that during these days of Lent he guard his life with all purity and at the same time wash away during these holy days all the shortcomings of other times. This will then be worthily done, if we restrain ourselves from all vices. Let us devote ourselves to tearful prayers, to reading and compunction of heart, and to abstinence.*
>
> *During these days, therefore, let us add something to the usual amount of our service, special prayers, abstinence from food and drink, that each one offer to God "with the joy of the Holy Ghost," of his own accord, something above his prescribed measure; namely, let him withdraw from his body somewhat of food, drink, sleep, speech, merriment, and with the gladness of spiritual desire await holy Easter.*
>
> *Let each one, however, make known to his Abbot what he offers and let it be done with his approval and blessing; because what is done without permission of the spiritual father will be imputed to presumption and vain glory, and not to merit. Therefore, let all be done with the approval of the Abbot.*

In addition to being a time of austerity, Lent is also a time of looking forward. Unlike the apostles, who grieved for the loss of their Savior, we have the benefit of knowing what was to come: the resurrection! We reenact this every year by observing austerity during Lent, and then increased joy during Easter.

As Benedict mentions, monks should be in constant austerity most of their lives anyway, but he realizes that few could really handle that. While I was in prison, the local Bishop had given all prisoners in his diocese a special "dispensation" for Lent. A dispensation is like the Bishop saying, "Look, I know that normally the rule is this, but I'm allowing you to bend the rule a little because there is good cause." The Bishop had said that all prisoners in his diocese did not have to observe Lent by "giving something up," but rather that our lives in prison were already an act of "giving something up." Indeed, only those who have been in prison know how much we give up when we go there.

However, the other side of Lent can be observed, and that is the "looking forward" to Easter, to the resurrection. If we are eventually getting out of prison, then we may look at our release as a kind of resurrection; our lives will be resurrected as if from the dead, and we will have to go through a lot to get them back on track, just as newborn babies go through a lot to get their lives on track! If we have a life sentence, we can look at Easter as a celebration of the freedom we may have finally found from our former addictions and problems. I am always amazed at the freedom I found in prison!

When the Lenten season comes, look forward to the joy of Christ's resurrection, and how He can show you the way during your own resurrection.

50

On Brothers Who Work A Long Distance From the Oratory or Are on a Journey

Occasionally, monks have to travel outside the monastery. Benedict discusses the way in which they are to perform their prayers, despite their physical distance.

> *The brothers who are at work too far away, and cannot come to the oratory at the appointed time, and the Abbot has assured himself that such is the case – let them perform the Work of God in the fear of God and on bended knees where they are working. In like manner let those who are sent on a journey not permit the appointed hours to pass by; but let them say the office by themselves as best they can, and not neglect to fulfil the obligation of divine service.*

Sometimes, we can get weary of doing the same things over and over. We may even try to invent excuses to justify skipping things that we know we should do. Prayer is no exception. The mind is ingenious at inventing excuses! Rather, a monk's distance from the monastery is all the more reason he should be praying.

When you have an excuse for not doing something that you know you should, think about the excuse and try to determine whether you are really unable to do the task, or whether you're just thinking of excuses to avoid something you'd rather not do. More often than not, I've found that I really could do the task. In the end, I accomplish a lot more that way!

51

On the Brothers Who Do Not Go Very Far Away

This is one of the more interesting rules, as it seems to make little sense on the surface.

> *A brother who is sent out on any business and is expected to return to the monastery the same day, may not presume to eat outside, even though he may be urgently requested to do so, unless, indeed, it is commanded him by his Abbot. If he acts otherwise, let him be excommunicated.*

I can remember listening to the other inmates who had gone to an outside hospital for surgery. How they would talk about the great food! The hospital food was even better than the food in prison, and sometimes the guards who were driving them to the hospital would stop for lunch and buy a burger for the inmate. It was such a nice gesture on the officer's part, and those few dollars spent turned into a quarter pound of beefy bliss.

I think there are two different issues being dealt with by Benedict in this chapter. First, having a meal with someone carries social implications in many countries and cultures around the world. It is a way of saying that you are in agreement, or in league with them. You are aligning yourself by association with them. When you don't know the person, there may be danger in doing so. For example, if a monk were to accept a meal from a woman, and it turns out that she is the town prostitute, imagine the locals talking as they pass by and point: "A monk from that monastery is eating with a prostitute!" It might reflect poorly on the monastery as a whole. In prison, there were rules about who could sit at the same table as someone else. I almost got "hit" (stabbed) because I sat down with a person of a different race. I was told that, had I taken food from them, they would have had to kill me!

Secondly, I think that Benedict was a little concerned about introducing decadence. Much like the prisoner on his way to or from the hospital, that food would be so good that, returning to the monastery and looking at the food in the evening, he might begin to complain, even if silently in his thoughts. "Why should I have to eat this garbage? Man, the food they had out there was so good!"

I was very fortunate to be imprisoned in a facility that had pretty good food. I rarely complained about it (once I complained because an adversarial group had prepared our meal, and thrown pieces of glass and metal springs into our food!). I remember specifically on Thanksgiving and Christmas that we would receive a nice meal, even with a little extra food, and I would hear complaints from the other prisoners! "We used to get more than this." "Last year was better." "This ain't no Thanksgiving dinner! That turkey ain't even real!" I would just smile and say, "If anyone doesn't want anything, feel free to pass it down to me." I would just think about the homeless people and what, if anything, they would be having for Thanksgiving dinner or Christmas dinner. Compared to that, I was living in luxury!

Times are a little different today, so I think it's good to enjoy the food you have, even in prison, and sit with anyone, even if you disagree with them. After all, even Christ ate with prostitutes.

52

On the Oratory of the Monastery

As I mentioned briefly before, the oratory is the place where the prayers are said in the monastery.

> *Let the oratory be what it is called, and let nothing else be done or stored there. When the Work of God is finished, let all go out with the deepest silence, and let reverence be shown to God; that a brother who perhaps desires to pray especially by himself is not prevented by another's misconduct. But if perhaps another desires to pray alone in private, let him enter with simplicity and pray, not with a loud voice, but with tears and fervor of heart. Therefore, let him who does not say his prayers in this way, not be permitted to stay in the oratory after the Work of God is finished, as we said, that another may not be disturbed.*

You might be thinking that when they want to pray, the monks just go into the chapel. In most monasteries, the oratory is actually a separate place from the chapel. The idea of having a separate place to pray is a good one. The chapel is really for mass, for the regular service. Prayers are certainly said there (one would hope!), but the oratory serves as a separate location just for prayer (i.e. not for services or any other purpose). Maintaining the oratory's purity from use for other things helps to maintain its sense of purpose and its importance. It is, in this way, holy and anointed, specifically set aside for a special purpose. As a matter of fact, the Greek word hagiasmos, which we translate as "holy" can specifically mean something that is set aside for a special purpose.

Our lives, too, are holy and anointed. We have been set aside by God as followers, and our place of prayer and meditation should be something that reflects that. In most prisons, there just isn't enough room to set anything aside. When we meditate, it is often helpful to begin the session by envisioning ourselves in a different place, a place set aside just for being with God. When I meditate, I often begin by envisioning myself going down some stone steps into a basement where I can be alone with God, and meditating there in silence. It really helps begin the session.

If you can't set aside a physical space for prayer and meditation, set one aside mentally. It really helps.

53

On the Reception of Guests

Monasteries receive guests often. I have personally been a guest of several monasteries. Benedict covers some guidelines on handling "outsiders" in this chapter. This is one of the longer chapters, and so I shall address it in parts.

> *Let all guests who arrive be received as Christ, because* He *will say: "*I *was a stranger and you took* Me *in." And let due honor be shown to all, especially to those "of the household of the faith" and to wayfarers.*
>
> *When, therefore, a guest is announced, let him be met by the Superior and the brothers with every mark of charity. And let them first pray together, and then let them associate with one another in peace. This kiss of peace should not be given before a prayer has first been said, on account of satanic deception. In the greeting let all humility be shown to the guests, whether coming or going; with the head bowed down or the whole body prostrate on the ground, let Christ be adored in them as* He *is also received.*

Having read a bit about exorcism, I really enjoy the sentence about satanic deception. I picture the Superior praying with his head down, but the corner of his eye watching the guest to see if they're writhing in pain as he prays! Perhaps I've been watching too many movies!

It also reminds me that the monasteries were somewhat cautious about who they let in. The same should be with us; we should be somewhat discerning about those we let into our lives. We can have friends of different opinions (and we should), but we all have met people who wanted to be friends and seemed to be wanting to make trouble at the same time. Like the Superior who prays first, and kisses afterward, we should get to know someone a little before we let them into our lives as friends.

> *When the guests have been received, let them be accompanied to prayer, and after that let the Superior, or whomever he shall bid, sit down with them. Let the divine law be read to the guest that he may be edified, after which let every kindness be shown him. Let the fast be broken by the Superior in deference to the guest, unless it is a day of solemn fast, which cannot be broken. Let the brothers, however, keep the customary fast. Let the Abbot pour the water on the guest's hands, and let both the Abbot and the whole brotherhood wash the feet of all the guests. When they have been washed, let them say this verse: "We have received Your mercy, O God, in the midst of Your temple."*

The washing of the feet is such a beautiful act! The Catholic Church celebrates Christ's washing of the apostles' feet on the Thursday before Easter. When I was growing up, we called it "Maundy Thursday," and the word Maundy comes from the same word as mandate. It reminds us of the mandate by Christ that we wash each other's feet.

Not only is the washing of the feet an act of selfless love, but it shows our humility to someone else. As you may recall, the apostles did not want Christ to wash their feet. John 13.6-9 says, "He cometh therefore to Simon Peter. And Peter saith to him: Lord, dost thou wash my feet? Jesus answered, and said to him: What I do thou knowest not now; but thou shalt know hereafter. Peter saith to him: Thou shalt never wash my feet. Jesus answered him: If I wash thee not, thou shalt have no part with me. Simon Peter saith to him: Lord, not only my feet, but also my hands and my head." We should all have the willingness of Simon Peter, and say, "Not just my feet, but my hands and head, too!" We should be willing servants to our guests.

> *Let the greatest care be taken, especially in the reception of the poor and travelers, because Christ is received more specially in them; whereas regard for the wealthy itself procures them respect.*

There is something special about the poor, perhaps because they have the greatest humility. Where I was incarcerated, the prison system provided for quite a lot, including food, soap, toilet paper, etc. Other "luxuries" could be purchased by those who had money, and it was particularly difficult for those without family or money to have to see others enjoying luxuries they could not, like coffee, shampoo, etc. Perhaps today, you might package a little of your coffee in a small plastic bag and slide it under the door of someone you know cannot afford any, or maybe something nice from the prison canteen. Don't let them know it came from you. Just enjoy knowing that you are giving a little back to God, paying your tithe to the originator of all.

> *Let the kitchen of the Abbot and the guests be apart, that the brethren may not be disturbed by the guests who arrive at uncertain times and who are never lacking in the monastery. Let two brothers who are able to fulfil this office well go into the kitchen for a year. Let help be given them as they need it, that they may serve without murmuring; and when they have not enough to do, let them go out again for work where it is commanded them. Let this course be followed, not only in this office, but in all the offices of the monastery – that whenever the brethren need help, it be given them, and that when they have nothing to do, they again obey orders.*

Benedict shows that respect is important, including the respect that the Abbot shows to the monks. The Abbot knows that guests will arrive at "uncertain times" (i.e. all hours of the day and night), and that it is important not to disturb the monks, and Benedict feels this is important enough to warrant the construction of a second kitchen. Respect goes both ways, and we need to remember that, especially when we are placed in positions of authority, respect to those who are working "under" us goes a long way.

Benedict also mentions the cooperation of the monks in helping each other complete their tasks, that "help be given them as they need it." How many times have we seen someone ask for help, only to be given the reply, "That's not my job." And that person, concerned about what their job is, might never expect to receive help from anyone else, should the need arise. This is not the way to get things done efficiently. When someone needs help that I can offer, I should offer it. And many times in my life, others have been there to help me as well. It makes for a more peaceful environment, and happier people.

> *Moreover, let also a God-fearing brother have assigned to him the apartment of the guests, where there should be sufficient number of beds made up; and let the house of God be wisely managed by the wise.*
>
> *On no account let anyone who is not ordered to do so, associate or speak with guests; but if he meet or see them, having saluted them humbly, as we have said, and asked a blessing, let him pass on saying that he is not allowed to speak with a guest.*

This rule may seem a little harsh and "exclusionist" but Benedict's concern is for the well-being of the monks. Perhaps his concern is that a conversation with an "outsider" might make the brother long for the outside and eventually leave the monastery. Other problems can arise from contact outside the monastery. A famous monk in the late 1960s ended up becoming romantically involved with a nurse he met while he was in the hospital. Imagine the harm that caused the nurse, who had grown to love this man with whom she could never spend any time. While it was a beautiful thing (as love always is), it may have caused the monk to question the nature of his devotion to Christ and the meaning of his relationship with Christ, and it also might have made him question the vows he took. In the end, he remained in the monastery, and went on to write many beautiful books.

I, too, have been in a similar situation. I was involved with a 12-step group, and there was a person in the group who seemed genuinely interested in sponsoring me. I kept distancing myself from them, and the situation eventually resolved itself. What that other person doesn't know is the reason I was distancing myself: I felt an attraction toward the person, and I knew that no good could come from a sponsorship that involved something more than a sponsoring relationship.

Sometimes in our day-to-day interactions with others, we may encounter someone who seems to be trying to avoid us, or perhaps they seem to be trying to create a bigger distance between you and themselves. Instead of jumping to the conclusion that the person doesn't like you or that you may have offended them, realize that the reason may be entirely different. It might be something you never thought of, and it might be best to keep things cordial.

54

Whether a Monk Should Receive Letters or Anything Else

This may sound a bit more oppressive than even prison.

> *Let it not be allowed at all for a monk to give or to receive letters, tokens, or gifts of any kind, either from parents or any other person, nor from each other, without the permission of the Abbot. But even if anything is sent him by his parents, let him not presume to accept it before it has been make known to the Abbot. And if he orders it to be accepted, let it be in the Abbot's power to give it to whomever he pleases. And let not the brother to whom it was sent, become sad, that "no chance be given to the devil." But whosoever shall presume to act otherwise, let him fall under the discipline of the Rule.*

It is very likely that allowing personal packages could have led to problems of jealousy, as I mentioned earlier in the cases of those who have nothing and have to watch those who have "luxuries" enjoy them. Whatever the reason, it seems rather unfair on the surface. However, if the monks were allowed to receive anything in the mail, there would be things entering the monastery without the Abbot's knowledge that might cause all kinds of problems. I can imagine people having food sent in, or magazines and books that are not conducive to one's spiritual growth. Thus, the Abbot needs to ensure that the environment of the monastery is for the spiritual benefit of all the monks.

Likewise, we have to be vigilant about what we allow

ourselves to "receive" by reading or whatever. In prison, it was rare to see anyone's cell with vacant walls, or for that matter walls that were vacant of pictures of women. And judging by the poses, I would say that the chances were slim that they were pictures of family members! God has given us the ability to fantasize for our own good (such as my previous mention of visualizing quiet places before meditation). When we abuse that ability, we can limit its effectiveness in other areas. We can also cause other serious problems.

Some of you may have had drug or alcohol addictions in the past. Did you know that the brain can become addicted to visualizations as well? And they are much harder to kick, because unlike the situation with drugs and alcohol, these visualizations are always with you, in your head, so that there is no way to separate yourself from them. Imagine trying to fight a drug or alcohol addiction with the drug or a bottle strapped to your chest at all times, just ready for the taking. It would be nearly impossible!

For that reason, we need to be cautious about what we "take in" whether as drugs, alcohol, or even visually.

55

On the Clothing and the Shoes of the Brethren

I never envied shoes until I had been to prison. Benedict discusses the clothing and shoes of monks. This is a somewhat lengthy chapter, so I will discuss it in sections.

> *Let clothing be given to the brethren according to the circumstances of the place and the nature of the climate in which they live, because in cold regions more is needed, while in warm regions less. This consideration, therefore, rests with the Abbot. We believe, however, that for a temperate climate a cowl and a tunic for each monk are sufficient, – a woolen cowl for winter and a thin or worn one for summer, and a scapular for work, and stockings and shoes as covering for the feet. Let the monks not worry about the color or the texture of all these things, but let them be such as can be bought more cheaply. Let the Abbot, however, look to the size, that these garments are not too small, but fitted for those who are to wear them.*

When I first went to prison, we were issued blue dress shirts with buttons, regular zippered jeans, and nice shoes with Velcro fasteners (among other things). As time went on during my stay, the economy changed, and those items were replaced with cheaper items: the dress shirts lost the buttons and gained snaps, then eventually were replaced with simple pull-over shirts not unlike hospital scrubs; the jeans became pull-on, elastic banded pants, also not unlike hospital scrubs; and the shoes became much cheaper, lace up cardboard reinforced shoes with soles that lasted about a month or so (and that is if you didn't do any track running to keep in shape!). As these things changed, we started hoarding the older items, repairing them as we could, to keep the older and better items around. We would save them for family visits, as it was much nicer to see your family wearing a button up shirt than a hospital scrub pull-over.

We were also allowed to purchase clothing from certain outside vendors, if we had money. Those of us without a lot of money learned that the clothing was not as important as the person, and we began to see each other for who we were regardless of how we were dressed (or because of the fact that most of us were dressed the same!)

Thus, being dressed this way, all in common, really kept me from making judgments about other people based on how they were dressed. I was forced to look at their faces instead of their clothing, and I began to see them as individual people much more clearly.

> *Let those who receive new clothes always return the old ones, to be put away in the wardrobe for the poor. For it is sufficient for a monk to have two tunics and two cowls, for wearing at night and for washing. Hence, what is over and above is superfluous and must be taken away. So, too, let them return stockings and whatever is old, when they receive anything new.*

I recall being in "the hole" (known as "administrative segregation" or "ad-seg" for short), and we were allowed only two pairs of boxer shorts (underwear) for a whole week. We had to wash them in the sink in order to keep them fresh. At the end of the first week, the officers came by to exchange the clothing, so I stripped down to my boxers and handed them my old clothes. They only handed one pair of boxers back because I was wearing the other pair. I asked them why I couldn't get two pairs, and they said that I would only get what I turned in. Well, not to be outdone by their rules, and in dire need of fresh clothing, I took off my boxers to hand to them. I guess they weren't expecting me to do that! They quickly threw another pair at me and took off laughing! I found out later that most people just turned in one pair a week. Well, I figured as long as they are going to limit me to two boxers, they're going to have to see me in my natural form! The following week, after I went to the shower, I returned to find that the officers had searched my cell, and they had left a little present for me: an extra pair of boxers! I can't blame them. I wouldn't want to have to see me that way, either. It really makes me appreciate my underwear.

Let those who are sent out on a journey receive trousers from the wardrobe, which, on their return, they will replace there, washed. The cowls and the tunics should also be a little better than the ones they usually wear, which they received from the wardrobe when they set out on a journey, and give back when they return.

For their bedding, let a straw mattress, a blanket, a coverlet, and a pillow be sufficient.

There was a serious prison overcrowding problem when I was there. The administration had taken the tables out of our dormitory recreation rooms and replaced them with metal bunk beds. During the winter, it got very cold down there, where there was little heating. One winter, there was a new inmate who looked like a small child, he was so thin. He was on the top bunk, so everyone in the dormitory could see him shivering all night long.

During the night, I spotted one of the other inmates sneak up to his bed and give him one of their blankets. We were only allowed two blankets, and they had so many holes in them that they were rather insufficient for the cold. This other inmate had given up one of his precious blankets, leaving him with only one, to give to this young newcomer, who now had three and finally stopped shivering. That simple act of giving really made me see in a whole new light the inmate who had given up the blanket. Even the most hardened criminals can sometimes show compassion.

> *These beds must, however, be frequently examined by the Abbot, to prevent personal goods from being found. And if anything should be found with anyone that he did not receive from the Abbot, let him fall under the severest discipline.*

Don't ever think that hiding things in the bed is something new. Apparently, it's been done since the fifth century!

> *And that this vice of private ownership may be cut off by the root, let everything necessary be given by the Abbot; namely, cowl, tunic, stockings, shoes, girdle, knife, pen, needle, towel, writing tablet; that all assumption of need may be removed. In this connection, however, let the following sentence from the Acts of the Apostles always be kept in mind by the Abbot: "And distribution was made to every man according as he had need." In this manner, therefore, let the Abbot also have regard for the infirmities of the needy, not for the bad will of the envious. Yet in all his decisions, let the Abbot think of God's retribution.*

Private ownership in this sense is about things that should be shared among the community. The brethren are to live as brethren, as a family, and in that sense, what belongs to one belongs to all. No individual is seen as more special than anyone else. Thus, every item should be given to the community to benefit all, instead of only benefiting one person. That is why Benedict sees private ownership as such a bad thing here, as a "vice."

Likewise, there are some things in a prison that are for the good of all. There was an incident when someone in the dormitory had stolen the cable from the day room TV to use for his own personal TV. He was almost killed when people discovered who had done it. His error, other than thievery, was to consider the property of the community as his personal property. And that, I believe, is the vice that Benedict is attempting to avoid by preventing private ownership in the monastery.

When we come into this world, we own nothing. After we leave, we shall also own nothing. Everything here is on temporary loan, and we should never forget that. Even our clothes and shoes.

56

On the Abbot's Table

One of the privileges an Abbot can bestow on people is to eat with them.

> *Let the Abbot's table always be with the guests and travelers. When, however, there are no guests, let it be in his power to invite any of the brothers he desires. Let him provide, however, that one or two of the seniors always remain with the brothers for the sake of discipline.*

I mentioned before the social implications of eating a meal with someone. It shows an alliance or agreement between the two people. Benedict has expressed that the Abbot can eat with any of the brethren. This allows the Abbot to develop a closer relationship with the brethren. The fact that the Abbot does not appear to eat with all of the monks makes this a special appointment, to be chosen to eat with the Abbot. Thus, the Abbot may see that a certain monk needs a little encouragement, and may invite him to eat with him. That simple act may encourage the monk, knowing that he was chosen by the Abbot.

Feeling "chosen" can really make a person feel good about themselves. As a child, I was adopted, and I often had to deal with feelings of rejection. Later I realized that, rather than being rejected, I was chosen. My adoptive parents actually chose me. It's better than being picked first for a baseball team!

God, the Abbot of all, has chosen each of us. That is why we are alive. He also wants us to choose Him. In Luke 22.29-30, Jesus says: "And I dispose to you, as my Father hath disposed to me, a kingdom; That you may eat and drink at my table, in my kingdom: and may sit upon thrones, judging the twelve tribes of Israel."He is asking you to sit at the table with Him, to dine with Him. What a privilege! Live your life today as one of the chosen!

57

On the Artists of the Monastery

Quite a few monasteries have monks who do various craft work for the monastery, either for sale to the public, or to support churches or other monasteries.

> *If there are skilled workmen in the monastery, let them work at their art in all humility, if the Abbot gives his permission. But if anyone of them should grow proud by reason of his art, in that he seems to confer a benefit on the monastery, let him be removed from that work and not return to it, unless after he has humbled himself, the Abbot again orders him to do so. But if any of the work of the artists is to be sold, let them, through whose hands the transaction must pass, see to it, that they do not presume to practice any fraud on the monastery. Let them always be mindful of Ananias and Saphira, lest, perhaps, the death which these suffered in the body, they and all who practice any fraud in things belonging to the monastery suffer in the soul. On the other hand, as regards the prices of these things, let not the vice of greed creep in, but let it always be given a little cheaper than it can be given by those who are not monks, "That God May Be Glorified in All Things."*

There are two Ananias's mentioned in the Bible, but the incident referred to here is the one with the Ananias who was married to Saphira (or in some texts it is spelled Sapphira). This is in Acts 5.1-10, and the story goes like this:

> *But a certain man named Ananias, with Saphira his wife, sold a piece of land, And by fraud kept back part of the price of the*

land, his wife being privy thereunto: and bringing a certain part of it, laid it at the feet of the apostles. But Peter said: Ananias, why hath Satan tempted thy heart, that thou shouldst lie to the Holy Ghost, and by fraud keep part of the price of the land? Whilst it remained, did it not remain to thee? and after it was sold, was it not in thy power? Why hast thou conceived this thing in thy heart? Thou hast not lied to men, but to God. And Ananias hearing these words, fell down, and gave up the ghost. And there came great fear upon all that heard it.

And the young men rising up, removed him, and carrying him out, buried him. And it was about the space of three hours after, when his wife, not knowing what had happened, came in. And Peter said to her: Tell me, woman, whether you sold the land for so much? And she said: Yea, for so much. And Peter said unto her: Why have you agreed together to tempt the Spirit of the Lord? Behold the feet of them who have buried thy husband are at the door, and they shall carry thee out. Immediately she fell down before his feet, and gave up the ghost. And the young men coming in, found her dead: and carried her out, and buried her by her husband.

The sin of these two was not that they kept some of the money, but rather that they said they were giving all of the money, but actually kept some of it. They lied. Benedict refers to this because he knows there are people who would try to defraud a church or a monastery. I've even heard some guys talking about how they would go into the church and steal the money in the box for devotional candles in order to support their drug habit!

Craftsmen can become quite proud of their work, and that can often be detrimental in the monastery. Though some monks may be very good at making statues, paintings, or other art, other monks contribute in their own way, and no monk should see his work as more important than another's. The same holds true for those of us living outside the monastery. How unappreciated are secretaries, often seen as "below" managers and other office personnel. If it weren't for the work they do, half the managers couldn't do their jobs! Try not to let yourself think that the work you do is any more important than the work others do, especially in prison.

All the inmates who work in prison are trying to make things run for the benefit of everyone. Take some time to appreciate the work of others that often goes unnoticed. The guys who work in the laundry, having to deal with everyone's dirty clothes all the time; the kitchen workers who have to cook large quantities of food in a short amount of time, as well as those who clean the trays; the clerks who do all the paperwork to make sure cell moves and other things happen; the porters and yard workers who clean the yard and the housing units. All these people, and many others, affect the way you live in prison each day. And more often than not, someone always thinks their job is more important than these people. Try to imagine what would happen if the laundry shut down, or the kitchen. What would the building look like if the porters didn't clean it? Now, you may be able to appreciate their jobs a little more.

58

On the Manner *of* Admitting Brothers

It is vitally important that the monastery ensure those who are seeking to become monks are really meant to do so. In this chapter, Benedict discusses how a monk joins the monastery. This is another rather lengthy chapter, so I will break it down into parts, as usual.

> *Let easy admission not be given to one who newly comes to change his life; but, as the Apostle said, "Test the spirits, whether they are of God." If, therefore, the newcomer keeps on knocking, and after four or five days it is seen that he patiently bears the harsh treatment offered him and the difficulty of admission, and that he perseveres in his request, let admission be granted him, and let him live for a few days in the apartment of the guests.*

This always reminds me of the hazing of college students seeking admission to a fraternity. The testing of the spirit is designed to determine whether a monk has truly been called to the monastery. It is unfortunately common that monks join a monastery, only to leave shortly afterward because the monastic life is difficult. It is not meant for everyone, much like the military life.

Many inmates in prison were or are members of gangs, either gangs from "the streets" or prison gangs. Most of those gangs have requirements for someone to join their gang. Unfortunately, it is often the killing of a rival gang member. The gangs do this to test the person's loyalty to them. The army tests to ensure that the soldier will be ready for combat. The monastery tests for both of these reasons.

> *But afterward let him live in the apartment of novices, and there let him meditate, eat, and sleep. Let a senior also be appointed for him, who is qualified to win souls, who will observe him with great care and see whether he really seeks God, whether he is eager for the Work of God, obedience and humiliations. Let him be shown all the hard and rugged things through which we pass on to God.*
>
> *If he promises to remain steadfast, let this Rule be read to him in order after the lapse of two months, and let it be said to him: Behold the law under which you desire to combat. If you can keep it, enter; if, however, you cannot, depart freely. If he still perseveres, then let him be taken back to the aforesaid apartment of the novices, and let him be tried again in all patience. And after the lapse of six months let the Rule be read over to him, that he may know for what purpose he enters. And if he still remains firm, let the same Rule be read to him again after four months.*

A novice is one of the "ranks" of a monk. When they first request to enter the monastery, they are called a "postulant." Then, after a few months, they enter the novitiate as a "novice." After some time, they will make their final vows and be received by the community.

Benedict is careful to point out all the rules and regulations to the new monks so that they know what they're getting into. We may wish that someone had explained to us all that we were getting into when we got "caught up" in our crime. When you are released, you may want to dedicate some of your time to speaking to groups about life in prison and how they can change their lives to avoid prison. There are lots of programs run by various police agencies that work with wild, unruly, and "troubled" youth, and you may be able to offer something that no officer can: a glimpse of what life in prison is really like.

And if, after having weighed the matter with himself he promises to keep everything, and to do everything that is commanded him, then let him be received into the community, knowing that he is now placed under the law of the Rule, and that from that day forward it is no longer permitted to him to pull away his neck from under the yoke of the Rule, which after so long a deliberation he was at liberty either to refuse or to accept.

Vows are very serious things, and when we make a vow to God, it should be taken very seriously indeed. It's like keeping your word and doing what you say you are going to do. Your word reflects on your character. I had lots of people in prison say to me, "I give you my word." Big deal! I didn't know who they were. All I knew was that they were convicted felons like me, so their word meant very little to me, especially since I had seen so many people say that and then later go back on their word. That shows that their word was worthless to begin with! When you promise to do something, carry it through no matter what. If you are not sure you can carry it through, don't make the promise. That way, your word will be worth something.

Let him who is received promise in the oratory, in the presence of all, before God and His saints, stability, the conversion of morals, and obedience, in order that, if he should ever do otherwise, he may know that he will be condemned by God "Whom he mocks." Let him make a written statement of his promise in the name of the saints whose relics are there, and of the Abbot there present. Let him write this document with his own hand; or at least, if he does not know how to write, let another write it at his request, and let the novice make his mark, and with his own hand place it on the altar. When he has placed it there, let the novice next begin the verse: "Uphold me, O Lord, according to Your word and I shall live; and let me not be confounded in my expectations." Then let all the brotherhood repeat this verse three times, adding the "Glory to the Father.*"*

Then let that novice brother cast himself down at the feet of all, that they may pray for him; and from that day let him be counted in the brotherhood.

Though I am only an Oblate (a monk who lives outside the monastery), I also took the same three vows described here: stability, conversion (reformation of life), and obedience. It may seem difficult to make such a vow to another person. After all, we were probably taught that it was good to "be your own man" and never to let anyone else rule over you. However, if you are in prison, you should come to the realization that whatever you were doing before didn't work out all that well! I realized that I did not belong in the driver's seat of my life.

I am not saying that we should become slaves to the whims of another person. Rather, I think that we should exercise our freedom in a responsible way, and since we (as prisoners) apparently aren't that good at doing things in a responsible way, why not use a guideline to help us out. Isn't that what the Rule of Benedict is all about?

If he has any property, let him first either dispose of it to the poor or bestow it on the monastery by a formal donation, reserving nothing for himself as indeed he should know that from that day onward he will no longer have power even over his own body.

Let him, therefore, be divested at once in the oratory of the garments with which he is clothed, and be vested in the garb of the monastery. But let the clothes of which he was divested be stored in the wardrobe to be preserved, that, if on the devil's persuasion he should ever consent to leave the monastery (which God forbid) he be then stripped of his monastic habit and cast

> *out. But let him not receive the document of his profession which the Abbot took from the altar, but let it be preserved in the monastery.*

The first sentence of this last paragraph covers the other two vows that monastics take: poverty and chastity (the latter being disclosed in the statement that he will "no longer have power even over his own body.") I find the idea of the former clothes sitting in the monastery a little daunting. They would be there as a constant reminder that you are free to leave should you decide. As an alcoholic, that would be like putting a bottle in the cupboard up high: I would know that it's there, and it would be always on my mind letting me know that I am free to return to that lifestyle should I so choose.

There have been times in my recovery when I have been tempted to return to drinking. Thankfully, I have not gone back. But I know, like that bottle in the cupboard, that the line I walk between sobriety and drunkenness is a very thin one, and it wouldn't take much for me to cross it. The same is true of other addictions as well as returning to a life of crime. When you are on parole, you will be short on money, maybe short on food, and the life of crime will look very attractive again. That is why this time is called parole: it is a promise that you make that, under trial, through a test to see how you will do under even some of the worst circumstances, you will do the right thing. That is also my prayer for you.

59

On the Children of the Noble and of the Poor Who Are Offered

Just like prison, monasteries have people from all walks of life. Benedict discusses how to receive the children of the wealthy and the poor as monks.

> *If it happens that a nobleman offers his son to God in the monastery and the boy is of tender age, let his parents execute the written promise which we have mentioned above; and with the oblation let them wrap that document and the boy's hand in the altar cloth and thus offer him.*
>
> *As to their property, let them bind themselves under oath in the same document that they will never give him anything themselves nor through any other person, nor in any way whatever, nor leave a chance for his owning anything; or else, if they refuse to do this and want to make an offering to the monastery as an alms for their own benefit, let them make a donation to the monastery of whatever goods they wish to give, reserving to themselves the income of it, if they so desire. And let everything be so barred that the boy remain in no uncertainty, which might deceive and ruin him (which God forbid) – a pass we have learned by experience.*
>
> *Let those who are poor act in like manner. But as to those who have nothing at all, let them simply make the declaration, and with the oblation offer their son in the presence of witnesses.*

If you have children, you might understand that parents who brought their children to the monastery would want to send them things to ensure that they were living well. But if that's the case, why did they send the children to a monastery? Certainly, they should understand that a monastery is not a place of comfortable living.

Benedict notes that he has learned these things by experience. He didn't just make up these rules to be some kind of cruel taskmaster. He has learned what causes people to stray from the life intended for a monk, and that's why he had written the Rule in the first place.

Sometimes, we might be subjected to rules that seem to make little sense. There are lots of rules in prison, and some of them don't seem to make any sense. However, many of the rules are there for a reason, and most of them are there because someone in the past did something stupid, and now there's a rule to keep that from happening again. Yes, sometimes the stupidity of one person affects a lot of people.

I used to have lots of inmates ask me to help them with legal work. One time, an inmate came to me and complained that a certain group of people had been barred from visitation only under certain circumstances, and he wanted to appeal it with the argument that the danger that the administration was worried about was present under all circumstances, so there should not be a rule saying that they can't visit these times, but can these other times. I explained to him that if he made that argument, the prison would likely agree that the danger was present under both situations, and would then bar visitation completely. I explained how it would become known that he was the guy who had made the appeal, and that there would be people lining up to bludgeon him with their fists. He saw my point and withdrew the complaint.

Sometimes, it helps to step back and take a look at the whole picture. If I decide to do something, how is it going to affect others? That way, I can begin to make more intelligent decisions. And keep from getting bludgeoned.

60

On Priests Who May Wish to Live in the Monastery

There is a difference between a monk and a priest. While someone can, in fact, be both, it is not always the case.

> *If a priest asks to be received into the monastery, let consent not be granted too readily; still, if he urgently persists in his request, let him know that he must keep the whole discipline of the Rule, and that nothing will be relaxed in his favor, that it may be as it is written: "Friend, for what reason have you come?"*
>
> *It may be granted him, however, to stand next after the Abbot, and to give the blessing, or to celebrate Mass, but only if the Abbot orders him to do so; but if he does not bid him, let him not presume to do anything under whatever consideration, knowing that he is under the discipline of the Rule, and let him rather give examples of humility to all. But if there is a question of an appointment in the monastery, or any other matter, let him be ranked by the time of his entry into the monastery, and not by the place granted him in consideration of the priesthood.*
>
> *But if a cleric, moved by the same desire, wishes to join the monastery, let him too have a middle place, provided he promises to keep the Rule and personal stability.*

The quote at the end of the first paragraph is intended to quote Matthew 26.50. It seems it doesn't really relate to the text, until you understand the context of the quote. The quote is from Jesus to Judas, just as Judas is betraying Jesus to the soldiers who have come to take him away. After the kiss from

Judas, Jesus says, “Friend, for what have you come?” In other words, what is your purpose in coming here? Benedict wants to ensure that there are no ulterior motives behind the priest’s admission to the monastery.

In essence, this chapter is all about setting expectations. When we set our expectations too high, we are more vulnerable to having those expectations dashed down when they are not met. When we set them lower than usual, then we will be pleasantly surprised when they are exceeded.

Christ gives an excellent example of this regarding the seating at a wedding (Luke 14.8-10): “When thou art invited to a wedding, sit not down in the first place, lest perhaps one more honourable than thou be invited by him: And he that invited thee and him, come and say to thee, Give this man place: and then thou begin with shame to take the lowest place. But when thou art invited, go, sit down in the lowest place; that when he who invited thee, cometh, he may say to thee: Friend, go up higher. Then shalt thou have glory before them that sit at table with thee.“ Benedict is saying the same thing; just because you’re a priest, don’t think that you can waltz in to a monastery and take the highest place.

Set your expectations appropriately. That way, if the worse scenario happens you’ll get exactly what you expected, and if anything better happens, you’ll be pleasantly surprised.

I am reminded of this when I first started meditating. The expectation was that something would “happen.” Nothing happened. It was only five minutes, and it was an excruciating five minutes that seemed to last for an hour! So I felt a little disappointed. In fact, what was supposed to happen did happen! Meditation is all about silencing the mind, and although my mind was a little noisy (as it always is), it was noisy because things were too silent. At first it’s as if the mind is afraid of silence, as if it thinks it will have to address its own issues if there is nothing else to concentrate on. So, to avoid having to deal with its own issues, it creates its own noise. Our job, in meditation, is to let the noise go by, like a passing car, and come back to the mantra. It is in the mantra that the mind will almost hypnotically become involved, and it will eventually become quieter, even if for just a few seconds. After years and years of jabber up there in my head, even a few seconds of silence is wonderful!

Make sure when you begin your meditation that you set your expectations appropriately as well. Don't expect "something" to happen. Rather, strive for nothing to happen. The nothing will be the silence, and rather than simply being nothing, it is the path to some pretty powerful stuff!

61

How Stranger Monks Are To Be Received

A pilgrim monk is a monk coming from another monastery. This chapter gives Benedict a chance to explain the vow of stability a little more. I'll cover this chapter in three sections.

> *If a monk who is a stranger, arrives from a distant place and desires to live in the monastery as a guest, and is satisfied with the customs he finds there, and does not trouble the monastery with superfluous wants, but is satisfied with what he finds, let him be received for as long a time as he desires. Still, if he should reasonably, with humility and charity, censure or point out anything, let the Abbot consider discreetly whether the Lord did not perhaps send him for that very purpose. If later on he desires to declare his stability let his wish not be denied, and especially since his life could be known during his stay as a guest.*

The vow of stability has to do with a monk staying in one place. After all, if a monk decided he didn't like the conditions at one monastery, or perhaps a group of monks were not happy with the appointment of a new Abbot, they would all flock over to another monastery. This would happen every time they didn't like the way things were going. You may recall Benedict referring to them in the first chapter as "Gyrovagues." Gyro is from a word that means circle, and vague from the Latin vagari meaning to wander. In other words, they wander in circles, unsure of themselves and what they really want (or need). Thus, when a monk becomes "attached" to a monastery, he will "bind himself to stability."

I spent the early part of my life moving around a lot, and I can tell you that it's nice to stay in one place for a while. Stability gives you peace, so practice stability in your life, and you will have peace.

> *But if during the time that he was a guest he was found to be troublesome and disorderly, he must not only not associate with the monastic body but should even be politely requested to leave, that others may not be infected by his evil life. But if he has not been like one who deserves to be cast forth, he should not only be admitted to join the brotherhood, if he applies, but he should even be urged to remain, that others may be taught by his example, because we serve one Lord and fight under one King everywhere. If the Abbot recognizes him to be such a one he may also place him in a somewhat higher rank.*

Those who are disruptive to the harmony of the community are politely asked to leave. We can take a look at our own community, our community of friends, and even our community of thoughts, and if we find something or someone that is particularly disruptive or "prone to vice," it may be time to ask them to leave.

I do not mean literally, especially if you are in prison. You can't simply ask another inmate to leave the prison. If that were the case, I wish someone had asked me! Rather, what I mean is that we may have someone in our circle of friends whose vices are causing you some difficulty in your attempt to turn your life around. If your friend's behavior won't change, it may be time to spend time with others.

Likewise, perhaps it's just not someone in your circle of friends, but some recurring thoughts or mental interruptions during meditation. I have heard some meditators say that when they get interruptions, they pleasantly ask the thoughts to leave.

> *The Abbot may, however, place not only a monk, but also those of the previously mentioned grades of priests and clerics, in a higher place than that of their entry, if he sees their lives to be such that they deserve it. But let the Abbot take care never to admit a monk of any other known monastery to residence, without the consent of his Abbot or commendatory letters, because it is written: "What you desire not have done to yourself, do not do to another."*

The simplicity of the Golden Rule! "Do not to another what you would not want done to yourself." If we could all live by this simple rule, I think our lives would be much better. Benedict's concern here is that a monastery might lose a good and useful monk to a neighboring monastery, resulting in possibly a little animosity between the monasteries. Additionally, one of the vows that the monk takes is stability, so unless he is really needed somewhere else, he really should stay where he is.

62

On the Priests of the Monastery

We have discussed the priests who wish to join a monastery, but an Abbot can also have some of the monks ordained as priests.

> *If the Abbot desires to have a priest or a deacon ordained, let him select from among his monks one who is worthy to carry out the priestly office.*
>
> *But let the one who has been ordained be on his guard against arrogance and pride, and let him not attempt to do anything but what is commanded him by the Abbot, knowing that he is now all the more subject to the discipline of the Rule; and in consequence of the priesthood let him not forget the obedience and discipline of the Rule, but advance more and more in godliness.*
>
> *Let him, however, always keep the place which he had when he entered the monastery, except when he is engaged in sacred functions, unless the choice of the community and the wish of the Abbot have promoted him in acknowledgment of the merit of his life. Let him know, however, that he must observe the Rule prescribed by the Deans and the Superiors.*
>
> *If he should act otherwise, let him be judged, not as a priest, but as a rebel; and if after frequent warnings he does not amend, and his guilt is clearly shown, let him be cast forth from the monastery, provided his obstinacy is such that he will neither submit nor obey the Rule.*

The problem with positions of apparent importance, such as the priesthood, is that they have a tendency to introduce an element of pride. As the saying goes, "power corrupts." For that reason, Benedict mentions that the priest is "all the more subject to the discipline of the Rule." The reason is that, if those in any kind of elevated position begin to go around the rules, it sets a very bad example for all the others.

In prison, it can be very difficult to watch the corruption among some of the officers and other prison officials. We feel so helpless to do anything about it, and it's very unfair. I remember when I first arrived in prison, we had a temporary warden. The reason was that the previous warden had been caught stealing food from the inmates' main facility kitchen, putting it in the trunk of his car, and driving it home. Imagine, a man making an enormous amount of money (over $100,000 US), stealing food from the state prison! His position made him think that he was above the law, and so he felt he could do whatever he wanted.

The problem is compounded by the fact that there is very little effective oversight in the prisons. There is no real way to monitor what goes on inside. When the state officials used to come visit the prison, they would detain the cars at the gate "for inspection purposes" and one of the guards would go inside and radio all the yards. Since they had a warning, the guards would lock down the yards so that the inmates would not be allowed to discuss anything with the officials, and so that there would be less potential for the guards to engage in brutality against the inmates. It was a very corrupt system, but that is unfortunately inherent in any situation when someone is given power over others.

Humility is a careful balance. It does not mean that you let people walk all over you and boss you around. It means that you have good self esteem, but are not prideful about yourself. You know that you are one of God's children, and that like any good father, He loves you no matter what you may have done in the past. But when you have balanced humility, you also know that no man is below you. It doesn't matter who that person is or what they may have done in the past, they are also a child of God, and that makes you brothers.

Where I was in prison, the standard issue clothing was all blue, so we used to say, "Everyone here wears blue." That meant that no one was above anyone else, no matter what.

63

On the Order in the Monastery

Previous chapters have mentioned monks maintaining their present order in the community, but not much has been said about what that order is or what it means. Benedict explains that now. I will cover this in two parts.

> *Let all keep their order in the monastery in this way, that the time of their conversion and the merit of their life distinguish it, or as the Abbot has directed. Let the Abbot not disorder the flock committed to him, nor by an arbitrary use of his power dispose of anything unjustly; but let him always bear in mind that he will have to give an account to God of all his judgments and works. Hence in the order that he has established, or that the brothers had, let them approach for the kiss of peace, for Communion, chant the psalms, and stand in choir.*
>
> *And in no place whatever let age determine the order or be a disadvantage; because Samuel and Daniel when they were just boys judged the priests. Excepting those, therefore, whom, as we have said, the Abbot from higher motives has advanced, or, for certain reasons, has lowered, let all the rest take their place as they are converted: thus, for instance, let him who came into the monastery at the second hour of the day, know that he is younger than he who came at the first hour, whatever his age or dignity may be.*

It can be particularly difficult for some people to work in a position where someone who is younger than they are is their senior. However, this happens. Again, this is a matter of humility. Often, someone who is younger has a more recent education and perhaps a better education in a certain area. For example, the prison yard where I was housed had a recording facility for the arts program, so that musicians could record songs, etc. I went to work there running the recording equipment. I had experience years ago in an old "analog" studio, where we recorded people onto different tracks of audio tape. However, that's not the way it's done anymore! Now, all recording is done digitally, and editing is a lot easier once you get to know the equipment. I had to take instruction from someone who had never worked in a recording studio before, because I did not know how to use the newer equipment. He had been running it before, so he was more familiar with it. While I had the experience of recording, it was a different kind, and the younger inmate had the more pertinent experience for the newer equipment.

In another sense, I recall when I first heard about meditation in prison. "Oh yeah, I've done that before," I said to myself. I had done a little meditation in high school. However, by opening my mind to hear about this meditation, I learned that it was different, and that perhaps it could make a difference in my life. Instead of assuming that my years of experience with meditation would give me an edge on "doing it right," I found that I had to learn it from scratch. It was only then, when I had the understanding that I knew nothing about this, that I began to learn.

When we think we know it all, we will never learn anything.

Children are to be kept under discipline at all times and by everyone. Therefore, let the younger honor their elders, and the older love the younger.

In naming each other let no one be allowed to address another by his simple name; but let the older call the younger brothers, brothers; let the younger, however, call their elders, fathers, by which is implied the reverence due to a father. But because the Abbot is believed to hold the place of Christ, let him be called

Lord and Abbot, not only by assumption on his part, but out of love and reverence for Christ. Let him think of this and so show himself, that he be worthy of such an honor. Wherever, then, the brothers meet each other, let the younger ask the blessing from the older; and when the older passes by, let the younger rise and give him his place to sit; and let the younger not presume to sit down with him unless his elder bids him to do so, that it may be done as it is written: "In honor preventing one another."

Let children and boys take their places in the oratory and at table with all due discipline; outdoors, however, or wherever they may be, let them be under custody and discipline until they reach the age of understanding.

Benedict requires that a great deal of respect be paid to the elders. At the time Benedict wrote the Rule, that was the societal standard anyway, but it is as it should be. After all, the "fathers" have gone before and been through more of the harsh monastic life than the juniors. Even if a monk comes to the monastery at a late age, there may be a much younger monk who is senior to him. Honor should be paid to the senior monk (in this case, the younger one) because of the experience of monastic life, not life in general.

The more we meditate regularly, the more experience we gain at quieting our minds, and the more control we have over our minds as well. Even a "bad" session helps us gain experience (and really, there are no "bad" sessions except a missed session!).

The same is true of life in general. The more experience we have at something, the better we become at it. So, physical age really doesn't matter as much as life experience. I met people in prison who were much older than I was, but had very little life experience because they had spent almost their whole lives in prison. In prison, they were senior because they knew the ropes, they knew how things were done in prison and I learned much from them there. However, when it comes to preparing oneself for a successful parole, they knew very little. In those cases, I got more from the older first-timers, because they had more life experience "on the outside."

I recall one of the prison counselors telling me that I needed to think more like an inmate. I replied, "I don't know about you, but I don't plan on living here the rest of my life, so I'd rather prepare my thinking for successful life on the outside." The administrators thought I'd never survive in prison with that attitude, but it was that attitude that got me through.

64

On the Election of the Abbot

In the previous chapter, Benedict noted that the Abbot is addressed as "Lord and Abbot." Obviously, that title can go to one's head, so Benedict has outlined some rules for finding the right Abbot, someone who hopefully will not let things like that go to his head. Again, this chapter is a little lengthy, so I will address it in parts.

> *In the election of an Abbot let this always be observed as a rule, that he be placed in the position whom the whole community with one consent, in the fear of God, or even a small part, with sounder judgment, shall elect. But let him who is to be elected be chosen for the merit of his life and the wisdom of his doctrine, even though he may be the last in the community.*
>
> *But even if the whole community should by mutual consent elect a man who agrees to ignore their evil ways (which God forbid) and these irregularities in some come to the knowledge of the Bishop to whose diocese the place belongs, or to neighboring Abbots, or Christian people, let them not permit the plotting of the wicked to succeed, but let them appoint a worthy steward over the house of God, knowing that they shall receive a bountiful reward for this action, if they do it with a pure intention and godly zeal; whereas, on the other hand, they commit a sin if they neglect it.*

Mistakes happen, and sometimes people don't always make the right decisions. As you can imagine, that can be disastrous in the case of an Abbot. Imagine electing someone to rule over the whole community, and it turns out that the guy is corrupt and starts changing rules, breaking rules, etc. Utter chaos would ensue. It's important that the monks elect the proper people to rule over their community.

Likewise, it's vitally important that we elect the proper "ruler" of our lives as well.

> *But when the Abbot has been elected let him bear in mind how great a burden he has taken upon himself, and to whom he must give an account of his stewardship; and let him be convinced that it is better for him to serve than to rule. He must, therefore, be versed in the divine law, that he may know from where "to bring forth new things and old." Let him be chaste, sober, and merciful, and let him always exalt "mercy above judgment," that he also may obtain mercy.*

Here are some excellent guidelines for a leader. These are the qualities that we should look for in leaders, and they are also the qualities that we should try to develop on ourselves.

> *Let him hate moral faults, but love the brothers. And even in his corrections, let him act with prudence and not go to extremes, lest, while he aims to remove the rust too thoroughly, the vessel might become broken. Let him always keep his own frailty in mind, and remember that "the bruised reed must not be broken." In this we are not saying that he should allow evils to take root, but that he cut them off with prudence and charity, as he shall see it is best for each one, as we have already said; and let him aim to be loved rather than feared.*

I love the analogy of scraping the rust off the vessel. We are the vessels, and only in love and care for well-being does the Abbot scrape off the rust. It may hurt a little, and it may even be very uncomfortable, but it has to be done for our well-being.

When we are seeking personal growth, especially through meditation, we will find that there are times when certain issues block our path, and we need to deal with them. They are most likely incidents from our past, and they may be very painful. They may include abusive situations that we didn't even remember until they came up. As uncomfortable as this may sound, this is one of the benefits of meditation. The clarity of mind will cause unresolved issues to come to the surface, and the reason they are coming to the surface is that we need to address them. Just like removing the rust from the vessel, it may be painful, but in the end we will be like new!

> *Let him not be fussy or over-anxious, harsh, or headstrong; let him not be jealous or suspicious, because he will never have rest. In all his commands, whether they refer to things spiritual or temporal, let him be cautious and considerate. Let him be discerning and temperate in the tasks which he orders, recalling the discretion of holy Jacob who said: "If I should cause my flocks to be overdriven, they would all die in one day." Keeping in view these and other dictates of discretion, the mother of virtues, let him so temper everything that the strong may still have something to desire and the weak may not draw back. Above all, let him take heed that he keep this Rule in all its detail; that when he has served well he may hear from the Lord what the good servant heard who gave his fellow-servants bread in season: "Amen, I say to you," He said, "he shall set him over all his goods."*

In prison, it seemed to me that everyone wanted to be some kind of leader in the chapel. The jealousies and strife, even anger, would ensue. I even remember one inmate filing a legal appeal against another inmate because he was told he couldn't rock back and forth when he was signing in the choir! And the guy who filed the appeal considered himself a leader of the Christians! That is the kind of ridiculousness that Benedict is trying to avoid by giving us the guidelines of a good leader, an Abbot.

As I look over the list, I see that all these good attributes are kind of daunting. I'm not sure I'd want the appointment if it was ever offered to me! After all, as Benedict points out, one has to give an account of one's actions as a leader. I wonder if all those newly baptized Christians in prison know that they are going to be held accountable for their actions? Knowing that, I think I'd be a lot more quiet. In humility, let's take an honest look at our leadership skills and realize that, if our faith had been all that strong, we probably wouldn't have landed in prison in the first place.

65

On the Prior of the Monastery

After having discussed the Abbot's qualifications, Benedict now moves on to the Prior, who is kind of like the second in command. Again, due to the length of this chapter, it shall be addressed in parts.

> *It often happens indeed, that grave scandals arise in monasteries out of the appointment of the Prior; since there are some who, puffed up with the wicked spirit of pride and thinking themselves to be second Abbots, set up a tyrannical rule, foster scandals, and excite quarrels in the community, and especially in those places where also the Prior is appointed by the same Bishop or the same Abbots who appoint his Abbot. How foolish this is can easily be seen; because, from the very beginning of his appointment, matter for pride is furnished him, when his thoughts suggest to him that now he is exempt from the authority of the Abbot, because "you too have been appointed by the same people who appointed the Abbot." From this source arise envy, discord, slander, quarrels, jealousy, and disorders. While the Abbot and the Prior are thus at variance with each other, it must follow that their souls are endangered by this discord and that those who are under them, as long as they humor the parties, go to ruin. The fault of this evil rests on the heads of those who were the authors of such disorders.*
>
> *We foresee, therefore, that for the preservation of peace and charity it is best that the government of the monastery should depend on the will of the Abbot; and if it can be done, let the affairs of the monastery (as we have explained before) be*

attended to by deans, as the Abbot shall dispose; so that, the same office being shared by many, no one may become proud.

Benedict is saying that it is best to have as few at the top as possible, because differences of opinion or even leadership style can cause problems with the monks. He is also saying that having a few deans in charge of certain things would be better than having an arrogant Prior in charge of everything. I grew up in a family of four children, and my parents each had completely different parenting styles. Of course, we had figured this out rather early on, and so we would actually use those differences to manipulate them. There were things we knew we could get from dad that we would never get from mom, and vice versa. This, of course, caused additional strife in their relationship. For reasons such as this, Benedict is saying it's best to limit the number of people in charge. Or, as the saying goes, "Too many cooks can spoil the broth."

If, however, the place requires it, or the brotherhood reasonably and with humility makes the request, and the Abbot shall deem it advisable, let the Abbot himself appoint as Prior whomever, with the advice of God-fearing brothers, he shall select. But let the Prior reverently do what his Abbot has enjoined on him, doing nothing against the will or the direction of the Abbot; for the higher he is placed above others, the more careful should he be to obey the precepts of the Rule.

The faithfulness of the Prior toward the Abbot will engender greater obedience from the monks toward the Abbot as well. Thus, it is important that the Prior show his adherence to the regulations.

If the Prior should be found disorderly or blinded by empty pride, or has been proved to be a scorner of the Holy Rule, let him be admonished up to the fourth time; if he does not amend,

> *let the correction of the regular discipline be applied to him.* But *if he does not amend even then, let him be removed from the office of priorship, and another who is worthy be appointed in his place.* But *if even afterward he is not quiet and submissive in the brotherhood, let him also be expelled from the monastery. Still, let the* Abbot *reflect that he must give an account to* God *for all his judgments, lest perhaps envy or jealousy should burn his conscience.*

As I mentioned earlier, power corrupts, and occasionally a person who appears to be a good candidate for the post of Prior later turns out to be the wrong one.

Note that Benedict does not immediately get rid of the Prior. Rather, he is given four chances to change his ways. Thus, though the transgressions may be serious, mercy is shown first in the hope that the transgression will be corrected.

When we lack mercy with others, when we act as the judge, jury, and executioner all wrapped up in one, we are acting in a totalitarian way, and we can expect to be treated in the same way. As Christ said in Matthew 20.25-6, "You know that the princes of the Gentiles lord it over them; and they that are the greater, exercise power upon them. It shall not be so among you: but whosoever will be the greater among you, let him be your minister."

66

On the Porter of the Monastery

The term "porter" here comes from the Latin word for door or gate, and it refers to the monk who tends the front gate of the monastery.

> *Let a wise old man be placed at the door of the monastery, one who knows how to take and give an answer, and whose mature age does not permit him to stray about.*
>
> *The porter should have a cell near the door, that they who come may always find one present from whom they may obtain an answer. As soon as anyone knocks or a poor person calls, let him answer, "Thanks be to God," or invoke a blessing, and with the meekness of the fear of God let him return an answer speedily in the fervor of charity. If the porter has need of assistance, let him have a younger brother.*
>
> *If it can be done, the monastery should be so situated that all the necessary things, such as water, the mill, the garden, are enclosed, and the various arts may be worked inside of the monastery, so that there may be no need for the monks to go about outside, because it is not good for their souls. But we desire that this Rule be read quite often in the community, that none of the brethren may excuse himself of ignorance.*

The last sentence sounds rather final, and there are some who believe that this was at one time the end of the Rule, with the later chapters added some time afterward.

The porter of the monastery is usually the first person a guest will see from the monastery, so in a way the porter represents the entire monastery. Also, just like in prison, the temptation may be there to stray outside the gate, especially when the gate is so close. For that reason, Benedict has asked that the porter be someone whose "mature age does not permit him to stray about."

This chapter is another one of my favorites, as I can just picture the porter monk seeing a guest arrive, and with such joy saying, "A blessing!" You may be asking why the porter would consider a guest to be a blessing, especially since the arrival of a guest would likely mean more work for the monk. As Benedict pointed out earlier, guests should be received as if they were Christ Himself. Christ has told us that how we treat others is how we treat him (see Matthew 25.31-46). Assuming one is a Christian, one of the great joys in life would be the opportunity to serve a Christ in disguise! It's like the boss showing up in disguise to check on the workers! Just to be sure you don't get in trouble for treating someone badly, you treat them all as if each one were the boss. And so, it is truly a blessing when a guest arrives at the gate.

When a stranger comes to your door in need of something, do you say to yourself, "A blessing!" If you are like me, then more often your reply is something like, "Not again!" But you see, it's not just that the person at the door might be Christ. He said, "Amen I say to you, as long as you did it not to one of these least, neither did you do it to me." In other words, when we fail to help the strangers at our doors, we are failing to help Him.

67

On the Brothers Who Are Sent on a Journey

There was a previous chapter that covered monks sent on short trips, so here Benedict covers those who travel further.

> *Let the brothers who are to be sent on a journey recommend themselves to the prayers of all the brotherhood and of the Abbot. And after the last prayer at the Work of God, let a commemoration always be made for the absent brethren.*
>
> *On the day that the brothers return from the journey, let them lie prostrate on the floor of the oratory at all the Canonical Hours, when the Work of God is finished, and ask the prayers of all on account of failings, for fear that the sight of evil or the sound of frivolous speech should have surprised them on the way.*
>
> *And let no one presume to relate to another what he has seen or heard outside of the monastery, because it is most hurtful. But if anyone presume to do so, let him undergo the penalty of the Rule. In like manner let him be punished who shall presume to go beyond the enclosure of the monastery, or anywhere else, or to do anything, however little, without the order of the Abbot.*

Again, I am reminded of the inmates who went out to the hospital and came back having had cheeseburgers. No one would want to go to dinner in the prison the night after having one of those delicious cheeseburgers from a real fast food place! Benedict is saying two things here: first, the monk that travels needs prayer for what temptations or whatever he may encounter while outside the monastery. After getting a little taste of life outside the monastery, the monk may want to leave!

He is also cautioning that monk not to tell the other monks what he saw, because the temptations could spread.

Just the opposite is the case in prison, but with some parallels. For example, many of my friends would ask to have people pray for them just before they paroled. The prayer was not so that they would come back wanting to stay (I hope!), but rather that they stay out. And secondly, the temptations of the world might lead one to come back to prison. So, in both cases prayer is needed. Take care when you leave the prison that the temptations of the world do not lead you back.

68

If a Brother Is Commanded to Do Impossible Things

How many times, after having been asked to do something, have I said, "That's impossible!" And yet, in reality, it is quite possible.

> *If any difficult or impossible tasks be commanded on a brother, let him nevertheless receive the order of him who commands with all meekness and obedience. If, however, he sees that the gravity of the task is altogether beyond his strength, let him quietly and seasonably submit the reasons for his inability to his Superior, without pride, protest, or dissent. If, however, after his explanation the Superior still insists on his command, let the younger be convinced that it is good for him; and let him obey from love, relying on the help of God.*

Sometimes, the impossible just looks impossible. Other times, it really is impossible. However, attempting the impossible is not always a fruitless task. Here is a brief example. It is said that Alexander Graham Bell, the inventor of the telephone, was initially unaware that he was inventing something new. Rather, the story goes, he had mistranslated a German paper, thinking that it said some scientists were able to transmit different frequencies across a wire for voice. Supposedly, what it actually said was that this group of scientists was able to send multiple tones for telegraph across one set of wires. In other words, multiple telegraph stations could share the same set of wires for sending Morse code, not voices. Well, up to that time transmitting voices was impossible. Alexander Graham Bell had no idea he was attempting to invent the impossible. He thought he was just reproducing an experiment already done in Germany.

When asked to do the impossible, think about the situation. It might not really be impossible at all. And besides, you might just invent something accidentally.

69

That in the Monastery No One Presume to Defend Another

Just so you know, this chapter is not about monks defending each other in street battles with other rival monasteries.

> *Care must be taken that on no occasion one monk try to defend another in the monastery, or to take his part, even though they be closely related by ties of blood. Let it not be attempted by the monks in any way; because such conduct may give rise to very grave scandal. If anyone oversteps this rule, let him be severely punished.*

The situation Benedict is speaking of is when a monk is being punished for disobedience, and another monk comes to defend him. If the second monk has some information about an incident, he can address it with the Abbot separately, but he is not to attempt to defend his brother to the Abbot. Otherwise, the door would be open to just about any kind of chaotic mutiny.

In a sense, too, this is about rationalization. When we have thoughts or actions that are improper, we have to undergo a form of discipline to rid ourselves of it. The second monk is something like a justification, like attempting to defend or justify our action or thought when it needs to be disciplined from us. It's a form of making excuses for bad thoughts or behavior. That's why it is not to be tolerated.

70

That No One Presume to Strike Another

Tempers can fly, even in a monastery. Benedict attempts to avoid that in this chapter.

> *Let every occasion for presumption be avoided in the monastery. We decree that no one be permitted to excommunicate or to strike any one of his brethren, unless the Abbot has given him the authority. But let those who transgress be taken to task in the presence of all, that the others may fear.*
>
> *Let all, however, exercise diligent and watchful care over the discipline of children, until the age of fifteen; but even that, within due limits and with discretion. For if anyone should presume to chastise those of more advanced years, without the command of the Abbot, or should be unduly provoked with children, let him be subject to the discipline of the Rule; because it is written: "What you do not wish to be done to you, do not do to another."*

The golden rule comes back again, and Benedict is talking here about controlling one's temper. It is easy to lose your temper, especially with young boys (anyone who has been a father knows that!). However, everything we do in the presence of a child is a lesson to that child on how to behave. Thus, if we tend to yell and lose our temper, the child will learn that yelling and losing your temper is what grownups do, and it's OK.

Many of us who have been to prison have a bad temper. Tempers tend to flare up not as much from anger as from frustration. When we feel we are losing control over a situation, then our tempers flare. When this happens, take a deep breath and remember, you are never in control. It is always God who is in control. If you try something and it doesn't work, then the answer must lie elsewhere. And if you feel like striking someone (or something), it's time to separate yourself from the situation. Walk away and take a few deep breaths. Maybe even repeat your mantra. It will help you center properly.

71

That the Brethren Be Obedient to One Another

We have read how the monks take a vow of obedience to the Rule and to the Abbot. Now we see that obedience goes further.

> *The brethren must render the service of obedience not only to the Abbot, but they must also obey one another, knowing that they shall go to God by this path of obedience. Hence, granted the command of the Abbot and of the Superiors who are appointed by him (to which we do not permit private commands to be preferred), in other respects let the younger brothers obey their elders with all charity and zeal. But if anyone is found to be obstinate, let him be punished.*
>
> *And if a brother is punished in any way by the Abbot or by any of his Superiors for even a slight reason or if he perceives that the temper of any of his Superiors is but slightly ruffled or excited against him in the least, let him without delay cast himself down on the ground at his feet making satisfaction, until the agitation is quieted by a blessing. If anyone scorns to do this, either let him undergo corporal punishment, or, if he is obstinate, let him be expelled from the monastery.*

Cooperation is important in any living situation, and a monastery is no different. In fact, it might even be more important because so many people living so close together can eventually get on one another's nerves! If you are in prison, you know exactly what I mean!

Every time I read this chapter of the Rule, I am reminded of what my brother and sisters (and myself) used to say to each other when one tried to tell another what to do: "You're not the boss of me!" That is an example of pure childhood rebellion! Of course, sometimes we were not receiving the best instruction from our siblings.

All the monks have to work together to make the community functional and efficient, just like in prison. For that reason, it is vital that there be cooperation. It doesn't mean you have to listen to what everyone tells you, but it does mean that there are times when you should listen to another. When I started working in the kitchen, I had to listen to the "old timers" tell me how to operate the dishwasher. I had no idea how to run that thing, and they certainly didn't give the new inmates a training course! They just assign you to a job and throw you in there. Without cooperation, there would be disaster (by the way, the word "cooperation" means to operate together, and that's how we had to run the dishwasher). And there were times when we had to go to the boss, our superiors, and tell them that there was someone who was unwilling to cooperate. We were not "ratting him out," but we were concerned for the safety of everyone, because one guy not cooperating can screw up a lot of things.

As we learn to cooperate with others, we will find that things go much more smoothly for us, both inside and outside prison.

72

On the Virtuous Zeal Which the Monks Ought to Have

Attitude can make all the difference between a good day and a bad day.

> *As there is a harsh and evil zeal which separates us from God and leads to hell, so there is a virtuous zeal which separates us from vice and leads to God and life everlasting.*
>
> *Let the monks, therefore, practice this zeal with most ardent love; namely, that in honor they go before one another. Let them bear their infirmities, whether of body or mind, with the utmost patience; let them compete with one another in obedience. Let no one follow what he thinks useful to himself, but rather to another. Let them practice fraternal charity with a chaste love.*
>
> *Let them fear God and love their Abbot with sincere and humble affection; let them prefer nothing whatever to Christ, and may He lead us all together to life everlasting.*

Zeal is that quality that makes someone eager to do something. It is an energy that drives you. You may recall that there was an apostle named "Simon the Zealot." He was portrayed in the musical "Jesus Christ Superstar" as having a lot of political zeal, and he tried to convince Jesus to attack the Romans! None of that is actually in the Bible, but some scholars do believe that there was a political group called the "zealots" during Christ's time, and that this particular Simon was a member of that group.

Benedict is speaking of a different kind of zeal, the zeal not for political vengeance, but for the love of others. Now zeal is not something you can simply decide to have. You either have it or you don't. However, you can grow in it, and this is a natural progression as you discover the joy of acts of love toward others. Then, you begin to want more of that joy, and that feeling drives you, gives you zeal! This is the zeal of which Benedict is writing, and as we grow in our faith, and perhaps with the assistance of consistent meditation, our minds become clear and we are able to feel that zeal for others because of the joy that is returned to us.

It doesn't come overnight. Benedict even mentions in the beginning of this chapter that the monks should "practice" this zeal. And practice, as we all know, makes perfect.

73

On the Fact That Not the Whole Observance of Righteousness Is Laid Down in this Rule

This is the final chapter in the Rule left to us by Benedict, and it is somewhat of a footnote on the scope of the entire Rule.

> *Now, we have written this Rule that, observing it in monasteries, we may show that we have acquired at least some moral righteousness, or a beginning of the monastic life.*
>
> *On the other hand, he that pushes on to the perfection of the religious life, has at hand the teachings of the holy Fathers, the observance of which leads a man to the height of perfection. For what page or what utterance of the divinely inspired books of the Old and the New Testament is not a most exact rule of human life? Or, what book of the holy Catholic Fathers does not loudly proclaim how we may go straight to our Creator? So, too, the collations of the Fathers, and their institutes and lives, and the rule of our holy Father, Basil – what are they but the monuments of the virtues of exemplary and obedient monks? But for us slothful, unedifying, and negligent monks they are a source for shame and confusion.*
>
> *You, therefore, who hastens to the heavenly home, with the help of Christ fulfil this least rule written for a beginning; and then you shall with God's help attain at last to the greater heights of knowledge and virtue which we have mentioned above.*

First, I want to explain the mentioning of "Father Basil." Who was he? The reference is to Basil of Caesarea, commonly referred to as "Basil the Great." Basil is often considered the father of eastern monasticism, and Benedict was influenced greatly by Basil, as well as by his Rule (yes, Basil also wrote a rule for monastic living).

The reference to "the Conferences and the Institutes" is to the writings of St. John Cassian, known popularly as Conferences and Institutions (or Institutes). The Institutions mostly discusses the organization and operation of a monastery. The Conferences mostly discusses our inner hearts. Specifically, the ninth and tenth chapters of Conferences discuss meditation.

In this chapter, Benedict is telling us that those who seek spiritual perfection will have to go beyond this Rule. This Rule is mainly for beginners, he tells us. He goes on to say that those of us who are lazy and ill-living will find these other works as a "source for shame and confusion." Indeed, I am shamed just by reading Benedict's Rule, so I'm fairly certain I am far from perfection!

We can look at perfection not as an immediate goal but as something that will be attained when we are finished with this life. It is much like meditation. As you grow and grow in your meditation, you will find an increased peace and clarity in your life. However, you will still have those little mental interruptions, those thoughts that pop into your brain to distract you. If those distractions ever went away, there would be no more purpose to practicing meditation, since in meditation we are simply learning how to deal with those distractions.

Conclusion

I hope you have found this commentary on the Rule of Saint Benedict helpful to you. If you are involved with Christian meditation, as I am, I hope that I have helped you understand how the Rule can help you with your meditation. If you are not interested in meditation, but are in prison trying to change your life, I commend you on your goal. It is a goal that I set many years ago at the beginning of my incarceration. I wish I could tell you it was an easy road, but in fact it was one of the most difficult things I have ever done in my life. Thankfully, I was introduced to the Rule early on, and it really helped me as I tried to live it in prison.

If you have not meditated but are interested in starting, there's no time like the present. The following section has some guidelines from the World Community for Christian Meditation. There are also some prayers from the community there, and the prayers should be said before and after each session, so that the light of Christ is present with you.

May God richly bless you, and may you find greater freedom than you have ever had before, whether you are in prison or on the outside.

– Peace

> "The important aim in Christian meditation is to allow God's mysterious and silent presence within us to become more and more not only a reality but the reality which gives meaning, shape and purpose to everything we do, everything we are."
>
> – Dom John Main, O.S.B.,
>
> Founder of the World Community for
>
> Christian Meditation

How to Meditate

Sit down. Sit still and upright. Close your eyes lightly. Sit relaxed but alert. Silently, interiorly begin to say a single word. We recommend the prayer-phrase, 'Maranatha.' Recite it as four syllables of equal length: Ma-ra-na-tha. Listen to it as you say it, gently but continuously. Do not think or imagine anything – spiritual or otherwise. If thoughts and images come, these are distractions at the time of meditation, so keep returning to simply saying the word. Meditate twenty to thirty minutes each morning and evening.

Opening Prayer

Heavenly Father, open our hearts to the silent presence of the spirit of your Son. Lead us into that mysterious silence where your love is revealed to all who call. Maranatha... Come, Lord Jesus.

Closing Prayer

(for meditation groups)*

May this group be a true spiritual home for the seeker, a friend for the lonely, a guide for the confused.

May those who pray here be strengthened by the Holy Spirit to serve all who come and to receive them as Christ himself. In the silence of this room may all the suffering, violence and confusion of the world encounter the power that will console, renew and uplift the human spirit.

May this silence be a power to open the hearts of men and women to the vision of God, and so to each other, in love and peace, justice and human dignity. May the beauty of the Divine Life fill this group and the hearts of all who pray here with joyful hope.

May all who come here weighed down by the problems of humanity, leave, giving thanks for the wonder of human life. We make this prayer through Christ our Lord.

*Note: You may pray the group prayer, even if you are meditating alone, because with a World Community of Christian Meditators, you are never really alone.

St. Benedict's Medal

The medal of St. Benedict is shown above (front side on the left). The writing around the front of the medal is in Latin, and translates roughly to: "May we be strengthened by his presence in the hour of our death."

There are lots of letters on the back of the medal, including a special prayer.

The four letters "CSPB" stand for "*Crux Sancti Patris Benedicti*," which translate to "The Cross of our Holy Father Benedict."

The letters in the cross (CSSML – NDSMD) stand for "*Crux Sacra Sit Mihi Lux! Nunquam Draco Sit Mihi Dux*!" which translate to: "May the Holy Cross be my light – The dragon never be my guide."

The letters around the circumference of the medal stand for a special prayer in Latin against Satan. The prayer in Latin is: "*Vade Retro Satana! Nunquam Suade Mihi Vana! Sunt Mala Quae Libas. Ipse Venena Bibas*!" They translate as: "Get behind me, Satan! Do not persuade me with your vanities! What you offer me is evil. Drink the poisoned cup yourself!"

The word at the top, "PAX" is my wish for you. It is the Latin word for peace.

What does it mean to be a Benedictine Oblate of The World Community for Christian Meditation?

Oblation is an ancient form of living the monastic wisdom in daily life in whatever circumstances you find yourself in, marriage, single-life in the world or monastery.

'Oblate' literally means 'one who is offered'. Originally in the Rule of St Benedict it referred to children who were 'offered' by their parents to the monastery for formation and education. When these children reached the age of decision they could chose to stay on in the monastery or leave and live outside. These who left would often keep close links to the monastery though. Later on it referred to lay people working in the world who wanted to be linked to the spirituality of St Benedictine by becoming associated with a particular monastery. These oblates are 'associated' with a monastery, perhaps visiting it as a spiritual home from time to time but on the outside.

The World Community for Christian Meditation is a different form of monastery - a monastery without walls. However it has many of the components of monastic life: community, shared prayer, study and a common work. In St. Benedict's vision these are all linked as a way of 'seeking God'. For us the meditator is a member of the community. Some of these members make a specific and personal articulation of this by becoming Benedictine oblates within the community.

The community as a whole, and the oblate community in particular, is composed of those who practice Christian Meditation as taught by John Main and who feel called to 'serve the unity of all'. They share this contemplative practice widely with others: for example with children, people in recovery, students, the sick and dying, the mentally ill, the grieving. The obvious place we share this common life and mission is through the many weekly meditation groups around the world. Groups meet in churches, homes, schools, universities, offices and prison. However the same community and teaching is found in the retreats, schools and seminars, held continuously around the world.

John Main is the founding inspiration of the community and the first thing an Oblate does is familiarise themselves with his teaching. The teaching on meditation is available through many books and CD's. John Main had a vision of 'a new monasticism'. He speaks of this in a collection of essays published as 'Community of Love' (Medio media 2010). It is a valuable text to see how meditation fits into the monastic tradition and the oblate way of life. The same theme is covered in the recently published 'Monastery Without Walls'- a collection of John Main's letters to the community.

Every monastic community has its leader and guide and Fr Laurence Freeman OSB, a monk of the Olivetan Congregation, is the Director of The World Community for Christian Meditation and of its Benedictine Oblate Community. There are national oblate coordinators in several countries. After a short period as a postulant the novitiate allows a time for deeper study and reflection with the help of a mentor, a fellow but more experienced oblate and meditator. During this time the novice becomes familiar with the

Rule of St Benedict, meets with the mentor, begins the regular daily prayer of the divine office and continues to practice the two half hours of meditation, morning and evening, with renewed commitment. After a retreat and discernment the novice may make final oblation promising to live in the spirit of the Rule and its precepts and to live and work for the well-being of others through the community.

The commitment of an oblate within The World Community is of course primarily to the two half hours of meditation. But their day has a 'strong moment' of prayer morning, midday and evening. An oblate also regularly follows some form of 'lectio divina'. Many reflect on a passage from John Main such as in his daily reading collection 'Silence and Stillness for Every Season' (Medio Media 2010).

Alongside the prayer Oblates sense being part of a community and foster this by going to retreats, schools and seminars. This is part of an ongoing formation – a commitment to what St Benedict called 'conversion of life'. To meditate together is also a celebration of our common prayer and oblates try to attend a Christian Meditation group regularly where possible. There is also a twice year issue of 'Via Vitae', the WCCM oblate newsletter. There are also 'Oblate Cells' which are small groups of Oblates (two is enough) who meet regularly to share some reflection on the Rule and its influence in their life.

Apart from the prayer and community there is the creative venture of living out the spirituality of St Benedict in our daily lives. Primarily that means applying it to the context of family, relationships, leisure time and the workplace, living a life of prayer and meditation though the commitments, opportunities and responsibilities of our life. The Rule needs to be adapted to circumstances in a spirit of obedience, stability and conversion of life. 'The tools for good works', as St. Benedict calls them, need to be used creatively. The way we live oblation and calling is unique for each person.

Many oblates are involved in the particular work of The World Community for Christian Meditation. That may be to help run a meditation group, to support one by turning up, to help organise local events, to support the community financially by becoming a 'Friend'. It is about offering our gifts where they can be used. This sense of 'offering' is the heart of oblation and it is made in the context of a commitment to a rhythm of prayer. One of the fruits of oblation is deepening friendships with other oblates and meditators. These spiritual friendships arise from a sense of common purpose and calling, a sense of being on a journey together and extends beyond the visible community itself.

The life of an oblate is essentially like all serious spiritual life, about freedom and joy. It is about the opening of the heart, what John Main called 'an infinite expansion of spirit. It is not just about falling in love but being in love. Thus St. Benedict writes in his Prologue to the Rule: "We intend to establish a school for the Lord's service. In founding it we hope to introduce nothing harsh or burdensome. But if certain strictness results from the dictates of equity and for the amendment of vices or the preservation of charity, do not at once be dismayed and fly from the way of salvation, whose entrance cannot but be narrow. For as we advance in the religious life and in faith, our hearts expand and we run the way of God's commandments with unspeakable sweetness of love."

For further information on the Oblate Community of The World Community for Christian Meditation please visit the Oblate page on the WCCM website: www.wccm.org

About The World Community for Christian Meditation

www.wccm.org

John Main founded the first Christian Meditation Centre in London in 1975. The World Community for Christian Meditation (WCCM) took form in 1991 after the seed planted then had begun to grow into a far flung contemplative family. It now continues John Main's vision of restoring the contemplation dimension to the common life of the Church and to engage in dialogue in the common ground shared with the secular world and other religions.

The present director of the Community is Laurence Freeman, a student of John Main and a Benedictine monk of the Olivetan Congregation. The International Centre of the World Community is based in London with centres in many other parts of the world. The Community is a 'monastery without walls', with both developed national organisation and emerging communities in over a hundred countries. A major building block of all this is the growing number of small, weekly meditation groups which meet in homes, parishes, offices, hospitals, prisons, and colleges. They form an ecumenical Christian community of diverse gifts and traditions.

Annually the John Main Seminar and the Way of Peace events bring meditators together in dialogue with other traditions and global movements. The Community also sponsors retreats, schools for the training of teachers of meditation, seminars, lectures, and other programmes. It contributes to interfaith dialogue particularly, in recent years, with

Buddhists and Muslims. A quarterly spiritual letter with news of the Community is mailed and also available online. Weekly readings are available by email and a growing number of online resources are being developed to help the spiritual journey with the help of the latest technology. This enables new initiatives such as the teaching of meditation to children, networking young adult spirituality and the contemplative dimension of the life of priests. Medio Media is the publishing arm of the community producing a wide range of books and audio-visual titles to support the practice of meditation.

Meditatio is the outreach of the World Community initiated to mark its twentieth anniversary. Coordinated from the Meditatio Centre in London a programme of seminars will bring a spiritual approach to key social issues of our time such as education, mental health, peace and justice, business, care for those in recovery and the dying. Meditatio is developing the use of technology in the work of spiritual renewal. It will also help with the formation of a younger generation of meditators who will serve later as leaders of the community.

The World Community for Christian Meditation:
www.wccm.org

Acknowledgements

The original text quotations and chapter subheads are printed in Anaktoria Bold, a Unicode Font for Ancient Scripts by George Douros, copyright 2009.

If you are interested in learning more about meditation, especially Christian meditation, you may contact the World Community for Christian Meditation at the following:

The International Centre,
The World Community for Christian Meditation
St. Mark's, Myddelton Square
London EC1R 1XX England, UK
International Office: +44 20 7278 2070
Email: welcome@wccm.org
Web: www.wccm.org